The Best of The
LAST DAYS
OF STEAM

An NCB 0–6–0ST shunting at Maesteg colliery in August 1970.

Colin G. Maggs Collection/W.H. Harbor

The Best of The
LAST DAYS
OF STEAM

Edited by COLIN G. MAGGS

BCA

LONDON   NEW YORK   SYDNEY   TORONTO

This edition published 1993 by BCA by arrangement with
Alan Sutton Publishing Ltd · Phoenix Mill · Stroud · Gloucestershire

CN 1207

Copyright © Alan Sutton Publishing, 1993

Half title page photograph: Driver George Hunt on 14XX class
0–4–2T No.1463 shakes hands at Yatton on Easter
Monday 1957 with W.E. Harbor, former goods checker
at Clevedon.
Colin G. Maggs Collection/W.H. Harbor

Typeset in 12/13 pt Bembo.
Typesetting and origination by
Alan Sutton Publishing Limited.
Printed in Great Britain by
The Bath Press, Avon.

Contents

Introduction

OVER A QUARTER OF A CENTURY has now elapsed since British Railways abandoned standard gauge steam, and during that time a generation has grown up which has missed the pleasures of savouring steam rail traction except on preserved lines. Those enthusiasts who keep such lines running have done wonders, for few people twenty-five years ago dreamed in their wildest dreams that there would be as many preserved lines with such a wealth of steam locomotives that we are able to enjoy today. Wonderful as these preservationists are, it is quite impossible for them to recreate anything approaching an all-steam King's Cross, St Pancras or Carlisle – there is just not the scope; similarly, although preserved railways now periodically run goods as well as passenger trains, these are necessarily infrequent and often relatively short in length.

The railway in Britain has shown dramatic changes over the last thirty years, for the days of steam were a quite different world. In the fifties and sixties steam was king except for electrified lines around the great conurbations. Since then electrification has been extended from London to Scotland along both East and West Coast routes; to Southampton and Weymouth. Diesel-hydraulic traction has come and gone, while diesel-electric locomotives, once a common sight at the head of passenger trains, have been largely displaced from these duties by self-contained trains of either the multiple-unit or HST variety, so locomotives today are mainly seen on freight duties.

Lineside observation was different in the fifties and sixties. Then, you could see an approaching train further away, perhaps several miles distant. Black smoke, or white steam would appear, often visible even if the train itself was in a cutting or concealed behind trees or buildings. From my bedroom window I am able to see part of the London–Bristol main line. Although I could not actually watch the train itself over a full quarter-of-a-mile as one end of it was in a low cutting, nevertheless the exhaust from a steam locomotive enabled me to time it over the distance. The demise of the steam engine has deprived me of this pastime.

Lying in bed at night I could hear a train 2 miles away pulling up the 1 in 50 gradient of the Somerset & Dorset line out of Bath and then speeding on a level stretch before once again getting to grips with the gradient.

Both the Somerset & Dorset and the steam engines are now gone, and today's diesels are quieter and their sound does not carry so far.

Steam locomotive cabs were more open than those of electrics or diesels and their crews more part of the countryside. A cheery wave from a lineside observer was likely to be returned by an equally cheery wave from the footplate or guard's brake van. Train crews today are encapsulated and isolated in their vehicles and feel independent of the outside world.

There was a wider variety of locomotives in steam days. When steam appeared on the horizon, or the distant sound of a steam engine was heard, excitement would mount as it grew closer and closer until at last it could be identified. Today's locomotive or train, if visible at a distance, can probably be identified immediately.

As well as depicting locomotives in the last days of steam, the pictures in this collection show a change which has taken place in the infrastructure of the railway. Although most of the stations in use today existed in steam days, they had a different character. Locomotives of those days created dirt, and that dirt made the stations dirty. Many station buildings are of creditable architectural worth, but could not be appreciated because of the layers of grime. It has only been the cleaning of stonework and brickwork in recent years that has revealed their glory. In steam days, multi-coloured bricks only had one colour – black. In steam days, stations which had train sheds were dark, dismal and dreary and it was not surprising that the trend was to replace them with individual platform canopies. Train sheds today are attractive and valued for their splendour.

In the sixties, country stations often had well-tended, colourful gardens, but city stations were bleak and colourless. Today some of those stations which used to have gardens are now without as they are unmanned and have no one to care for them, but urban stations are beautiful with flowers – hanging baskets, tubs set between the tracks and on the platforms. In the sixties, often a local pressure group was formed to keep a station open and then having succeeded, or failed in its task, was disbanded. It is most encouraging that today there are long-term support groups for some stations, or lengths of line, developing traffic by giving publicity and sometimes even making stations more attractive by maintaining station gardens. In steam days, bridges and platform canopy supports were usually painted one colour; today, they are attractively and imaginatively picked out in various hues so that their beauty is revealed.

In the days of steam most goods wagons were of the four-wheeled, short-wheelbase variety, designed to go round tight curves found in the many private sidings serving industrial premises. Only short wagons could use wagon turntables which gave access to some goods sidings laid in congested areas where conventional points were impossible. Today's goods trains usually carry the same item – stone, oil, or coal, for example – whereas thirty years ago many trains carried a mixture of items. In steam days smaller goods yards were shunted at least once daily by a pick-up goods, dropping off wagons and picking up others to be taken to a marshalling yard for onward transit. Today this scene has completely disappeared and shunting has almost become a thing of the past.

Many commonplace, everyday things in the railway scene of thirty years ago have vanished. The goods station has disappeared altogether as has its hand crane. Closely associated with it, and also the parcels department of the passenger station, were the railway-owned vans and delivery lorries, quite often of the mechanical horse and trailer variety which were the forerunners of the ubiquitous articulated vehicle found on today's motorways. Farmers' tractors were seen among other vehicles in railway goods yards collecting sugar beet pulp or fertilizers. Cattle wagons were plentiful on market days, ready to take animals off to their purchasers.

At passenger stations travelling safes could be seen taking the previous day's takings to the district office. Boxes of fish would arrive by passenger, or parcels, train and be left on the platform for collection by local fishmongers, the station cat helping himself to one or two. On the walls were displayed complete timetables of the various services from that station, whereas today's timetables mostly give just the departure time, and offer no information regarding stations called at en route, or the arrival time.

Tickets were sold from booking offices in booking halls, rather than from today's more user-friendly travel centres, but offered a wide variety of colour-coded tickets, sometimes in two or three hues which were far more exciting, interesting and collectable than today's print-out which is no more thrilling than the receipt given at the local supermarket. One lost excitement of the booking hall is the strings of handbills printed in colour on newsprint and offering a variety of cheap excursions, or inexpensive mystery trips by rail. Another vanished feature is the Holiday Express, whereby you spent each night at home, but for a week were taken to a different holiday destination daily.

Today, much more intensive use is made of rolling stock. Instead of coaches being removed to carriage sidings for cleaning after just one trip, there is usually merely a brief turn-round time at the platform prior to departure on the next trip, sometimes all too short a period if out-of-course delays have been experienced. Thirty years ago some passenger stock was used only for a few summer Saturdays and for the rest of the year stood idle – a highly uneconomic procedure. Today's freight wagons spend little time stationary, merry-go-round

trains ensuring their almost continual use, whereas in the steam era, wagons were shunted before, during and after a trip in addition to spending time waiting in goods loops.

New signalling methods have caused lengths of some quadruple track to be reduced to double, or double to single, while some double track has been signalled for two-way working thus allowing one train to overtake another travelling in the same direction. Nests of sidings, once so common, are now much rarer.

Mechanical signal boxes seen every few miles, have been replaced by MAS boxes, sometimes out of sight of a passing train. Telegraph wires – always the bane of a railway photographer, unseen in the viewfinder protruded above a locomotive boiler and marred an otherwise superb shot – have now been largely dispensed with. Track work, once so labour intensive with the ganger patrolling his length knocking in loose keys, is now generally carried out by machinery.

Back in the last days of steam there were more signs of the Big Four companies than today, such as headings on poster boards, tickets for destinations to which there was less demand, luggage labels, initials on axle boxes, and rail chairs.

In Northern Ireland, after the Second World War the situation was similar to that on the mainland. Just as British Railways was set up in Britain following Nationalization of the railways, so in the same year the Ulster Transport Authority was formed to take over railway and road undertakings in the province. The lines concerned were the Belfast and County Down Railway and the Northern Counties Committee, the latter having been owned by the erstwhile LMS. The Great Northern Railway (Ireland) continued to serve both Northern Ireland and the Republic. However, its poor financial state caused it to be purchased jointly in 1953 by the respective governments, which continued to run it as a separate enterprise until 1958, when its assets were divided between the UTA and the Coras Iompair Eireann.

In 1954 the Bangor line had the perhaps dubious honour of being the first line in Britain to be completely dieselized. Internal-combustion engines were not new to Ireland as narrow-gauge lines had used them, and in 1933 the NCC introduced a railcar driven by two Leyland 130 h.p. petrol engines. Nevertheless, despite this early start the last main-line steam engines to remain in regular service in the whole of the British Isles were WT class 2–6–4Ts used to haul stone from a quarry near Larne to construct a motorway along the shores of Belfast Lough parallel with the railway.

One way in which today's enthusiast, whether a mature man harking back to the past, or a young person who never experienced the reality, can partly experience the atmosphere of the last days of steam, is through photographs and it is fortunate that many people recorded these events on film. In fact, so many photographed these scenes that a wealth of pictures keeps surfacing from quite unexpected sources.

It was quite a difficult task selecting pictures for *The Best of The Last Days of Steam*. Should they be best from the photographic angle, perhaps literally a surprising angle, giving a startling and unusual effect? Should they principally show locomotives with perhaps a little of their train and other railway features such as stations, signal boxes and signals? Should only clean, steam-tight engines be depicted in order to give a good impression of these machines, or should they be shown as they often were: dirty, leaking and minus number, or name-plates? Should diesels appear in the pictures, or ought they to be carefully trimmed off? (Many enthusiasts during the last days of steam had strong feelings about diesels and at least one person known to the editor, rather than catching the first train to his home station, if it happened to be a diesel would wait until a steam-hauled train appeared.)

In selecting the photographs for this volume, the following criteria have been used:

1. To give a fair balance of locomotives from each of the Big Four and BR, trying to show their various types. A few pre-grouping engines are shown, but most of these had already been withdrawn by the very last days of steam. An effort has been made to offer a balance between the different areas of Great Britain, because not all districts were covered equally by photographers. Some parts of the country were less photographed due to being populated more thinly, not being in a popular holiday area, or not enjoying weather conducive to railway photography.

2. To show the characteristics of the last days of steam –

dirty engines, painted-on numbers, missing name-plates, steam leaking from places where steam should not leak; short trains; branch lines; rail tours and last day specials.

3. To show, in addition to locomotives, the infrastructure of railways during the last days of steam: the many patterns of semaphore signals and their supports; a wide diversity of rolling stock both passenger and goods; a variety of passenger stations – unfortunately very few cameramen took pictures of goods stations.

4. To show a variety of scenery: landscapes, townscapes; trains in stations large and small; locomotives in sheds and in the open, stationary and on the move.

5. To express changes in social history; for example, twenty-five years ago steam trains were used for transport to school, office, or holiday, rather than the car; people's clothing was different, while railwaymen's uniforms have changed much in the last quarter century.

It is intended that this collection can be studied again and again. Just as with a painting, you can come back and see fresh things. They are pictures you are invited to spend minutes considering and everything is not expected to be revealed at a single glance like a roadside poster.

Town Stations

A brace of Beattie class 0298 2–4–0 well tank engines made a triumphant return to their early haunts for the first of two farewell tours to Hampton Court on 2.12.62. Originally constructed in 1874 as part of a large order for 2–4–0WTs to work suburban passenger services on the London and South Western Railway, these two engines, plus another, were exiled to north Cornwall during the 1890s and remained there until withdrawal. Having set out from Waterloo, the two octogenarians, Nos 30585 and 30587, with steam to spare, prepare to depart from Surbiton on the final stage of the journey; both have been preserved.

David Fereday Glenn

Ex-Great Central Railway D11/1 'Large Director' class 4–4–0 No. 62668 *Jutland* of Sheffield Darnall shed stands under the wires at Sheffield Victoria, carrying express headlamps while on station pilot duty. This locomotive was withdrawn shortly after the photograph was taken on 13.8.60. The line from Sheffield through Woodhead tunnel was re-opened for electric services on 14.9.54, but services ceased on 18.7.81. Sheffield Victoria itself had closed on 4.1.70.

Maurice Dart

UNTIL THE 1960S TOWN STATIONS employed large staffs. Apart from passenger and goods platform grades, there were also office staff, and cartage staff, horses still being used at some stations for town deliveries until about forty years ago, motor lorries being kept for out of town collection and delivery. Much of the merchandise sold in local shops came by rail – groceries, meat, fish, clothing, ironmongery, dairy products, sweets, chocolates and tobacco. General merchandise arriving in wagonloads included building materials and farm supplies, the latter ranging from items such as fertilizer, basic slag, grain and seeds, to slabs of cottonseed cake and implements. Many stations had warehouses for storing animal foodstuffs prior to distribution as required to local farms. Distribution facilities were also offered for commodities such as chocolate and biscuits. The latter were in tins which, even in those days, were recycled by being returned empty to the factory for refilling.

Town stations usually had several signal-boxes, most of which were manned twenty-four hours a day, with 6 a.m.–2 p.m., 2 p.m.–10 p.m. and 10 p.m.–6 a.m. shifts. Some manual boxes were so busy that more than one signalman had to be employed to work the frame, as well as a booking boy to make entries in the train register.

Stations have now become less labour intensive. For instance, new stock has automatic doors which the train crew can check are correctly closed before departure, rather than slam-doors which need exterior checking for safety, while the provision of lightweight luggage trolleys means that much luggage-moving is of the DIY variety. It is also hard to believe in the nineties, that in the sixties quite a few stations were still lit by gas.

The railway was rather more flexible in the last days of steam. Instead of fixed train formations, as is the case today, if a large number of passengers turned up, extra coaches were generally available to be added by the station pilot, or even for an extra train to be run. If urgent supplies had to be delivered, a van could be

On weekdays the all-Pullman 'Queen of Scots' express ran each way between Glasgow, Edinburgh and London King's Cross. The Down service left London at 11.50 a.m., while the Up departed from Glasgow Queen Street at 11.00 a.m. Intermediate stops were made at Leeds Central, Harrogate, Darlington, Newcastle and Edinburgh Waverley, with the option to set down only being available to passengers for Falkirk on the 11.50 a.m. from London.

On 31.8.60 the Up train pauses at Darlington for a moment before proceeding past the almost new Metro-Cammell DMU. The 'Queen of Scots' is headed by class A3 Pacific No. 60074 *Harvester* of 55H (Leeds, Neville Hill). It had recently been fitted with a double chimney.

David Fereday Glenn

attached to the rear of a passenger train so that they arrived swiftly at their destination.

C.R. Rust, station-master at Bristol Temple Meads in the fifties, with fifteen platforms, 434 trains daily and 636 staff under him, described a typical day. After arriving at the station at 8.30 a.m., he quickly scanned his mail before seeing the Chief Station Inspector, Ticket Inspector, Guards' Inspector, Yard Inspector and Carriage Servicing Inspector. Rust then had a few words with his Chief Clerk. He saw to the departure and arrival of principal expresses, particularly the Down 'Bristolian', on which travelled ambassadors, high commissioners, MPs, bankers and industrialists, arranging which exit the VIPs should use, that their cars were suitably positioned and the police advised.

Rust then settled down to correspondence and clerical work. Connectional problems frequently arose because of Temple Meads' geographical position, and Rust or his inspectors often had to deal with the wrath of a passenger who could not understand why a train with three hundred passengers was not kept waiting for him or her.

After lunch Rust visited the East signal-box, and Dr Day's carriage sidings. West box was also visited periodically, and once a week he went to Malago Vale and Lawrence Hill Junction carriage sidings. He saw the afternoon Chief Station Inspector before retiring to the office to carry out more clerical work, then returned to the platform to see the departure of important evening trains. He then signed the rest of his letters, and had a short talk with his Chief Clerk before leaving at 5.45 p.m. but was continuously 'on call', as an emergency such as a derailment would require his presence.

Class A1 Pacific No. 60162 *Saint Johnstoun* of 64B (Haymarket) passes a diesel-electric-hauled train by Princes Street Gardens, Edinburgh, on 12.8.58. The position of the inside cylinder can be seen above the buffer beam.

R.E. Toop

With class A headlamps in position and steam hissing from safety valves and cylinders, Riddles' BR Standard 'Britannia' class 7 4–6–2 No. 70041 *Sir John Moore* begins to ease the 4.12 p.m. express for Cleethorpes out of King's Cross station on 18.3.61. Home-going commuters mingle with enthusiasts of all ages to witness the spectacle of a leviathan of the steam era rousing the echoes of one of London's railway 'temples'. In less than an hour the same platform would host the arrival of the Up 'Flying Scotsman' behind one of the first Type 5 'Deltic' diesel-electrics. *Sic transit gloria mundi . . .*

David Fereday Glenn

The gloomy but very atmospheric train shed at Liverpool Street station, London, depicted on an afternoon with two trains forming part of the famous 'jazz' service of local passenger services. The nearest locomotive to the camera is class N7/5 0–6–2T No. 69664 (Stratford), while in the background is class N7/4 0–6–2T No. 69604 of the same shed, with a Chingford train.

The noise of the Westinghouse pumps on these engines was a distinct and very familiar sound to commuters from Essex and Hertfordshire. However, when this photograph was taken on 22.5.59, D55XX diesel-electrics (now class 31) were beginning to appear, thus sounding the death knell for steam locomotives.

Maurice Dart

Rebuilt 'West Country' class 4–6–2 No. 34031 *Torrington* at Basingstoke with a Waterloo to Bournemouth express on 20.7.63. The wheels of this engine were not spoked, but had holes and recesses in their discs. Originally built with a streamlined casing, this was removed on rebuilding to give greater accessibility. The class had a high running plate, similar to those on BR Standard locomotives. A close inspection shows that each lamp bracket has an electric light, but during daytime discs were used. The smokebox door is an unusual shape.

Laurence Waters Collection / D. Tuck

On 23.12.66 rebuilt 'Merchant Navy' class No. 35023 *Holland–Afrika Line* waits at Waterloo to head the 1830 express to Bournemouth. Although without its nameplate and in generally dirty condition, the engine survived until the end of steam seven months later, by which time it had covered 941,326 miles and had the dubious honour of working the last steam train into Waterloo on 8.7.67.

This night photograph shows the effectiveness of the electric route lights, just one of the pioneering innovations on these Bulleid Pacifics.

A.J. Fry Collection

U class 2–6–0 No. 31803 at Basingstoke on 20.7.63. This locomotive has a deflector on each side of the smokebox to cause an airflow sufficient to prevent smoke drifting down and obscuring the driver's view. Notice the handrail near the bottom of the deflector, placed conveniently for an engineman to grab when climbing the footsteps. A hand hole is provided in the deflector itself for a similar purpose. The van to the right of the engine is for fruit. To the left of this vehicle is an advertisement for 'Livery & Bait Stables'.

Laurence Waters Collection/D. Tuck

N Class 2–6–0 No. 31831 at Reading South station on 3.1.65. The fireman is taking the opportunity to move forward the coal in the tender, preparatory to working a train to Redhill.

The concrete items in the picture – platform wall and edges, lamppost and station nameboard supports – were cast at the SR's own concrete works at Exmouth Junction. Beyond the engine, on the low embankment, can be seen the former GWR's main line.

Laurence Waters Collection/D. Tuck

On a bright spring morning a long train of wagons heads south through Leicester Central station on the former Great Central main line. BR Standard class 9F 2–10–0 No. 92094 of 16D (Annesley) has steam to spare as it rumbles by the island platform bound for Rugby Central and Woodford Halse, its work-stained appearance being typical of a freight engine of the period. The date is 13.3.62.

Following closure in May 1969, part of the GCR route north of Leicester has now been saved and re-opened as a preserved line as far as Loughborough Central.

David Fereday Glenn

'Jubilee' class 4–6–0 No. 45577 *Bengal* of 89A (Shrewsbury) leaves Hereford for Crewe and Manchester in the summer of 1963. Notice the mass of point rodding and signal wires to the right of the track. The white plate on the left of the right-hand lamp warns locomotive crews of the danger from overhead wires – the electrification of the West Coast line had already begun.

Laurence Waters Collection/D. Tuck

This locomotive had only another six weeks to run and so was very near its own 'last days of steam'. Originally constructed as the famous LMS Turbomotive, powered by turbines rather than conventional cylinders, it was in due course decided to rebuild it as a standard member of the class. Here, on 29.8.52, two days out of Crewe Works after this rebuilding, 'Princess Royal' class 4–6–2 No. 46202 *Princess Anne* stands at Crewe station, having just arrived with a Down express. The ramp at the end of the famous foot-bridge leading to Crewe North shed formed an excellent vantage point for the photographer, as the train was standing at the westernmost platform.

At 8.20 a.m. on 8.10.52 this locomotive, hauling an Up Manchester express, ran into the wreckage of a collision between an express from Perth and a local from Tring at Harrow and Wealdstone station. The damage was so severe that it had to be scrapped.

Maurice Dart

On what was intended to be the final day of the Somerset and Dorset line, 2.1.66, Bath Green Park station was the focus of attention, with the arrival and departure of a special train. After travelling north over the S&D behind two Southern engines, class 8F 2–8–0 No. 48309 then took over for the next stage of the tour via Mangotsfield. This Stanier locomotive stormed out of Bath with an impressive display of pyrotechnics in the damp conditions, passing the motive power depot and signal gantries. Although the fine terminal station has been retained as part of a supermarket complex, there was no reprieve for the S&D itself; the last trains ran on 6.3.66.

David Fereday Glenn

Salisbury, the former London and South Western Railway station, with an interloper in the form of 'Hall' class 4–6–0 No. 6900 *Abney Hall* of 82A (Bristol, Bath Road), which has just uncoupled from a service from Westbury on 8.5.54. Visible to the right is what was once the GWR Salisbury terminus which, although closed to passengers for many years, still survives, albeit partly as siding accommodation and partly as offices. The GWR had reached Salisbury as part of the Wilts, Somerset and Weymouth Railway, while Salisbury was just short of the midpoint on the main LSWR line between Waterloo and Exeter.

Kevin Robertson Collection / W. Gilburt

Ex-GWR 14XX class 0–4–2T No. 1451 at Exeter St David's in July 1962 with an auto-train for Dulverton. The engine pushed its train in the outwards direction, the driver controlling it from a special vestibule in the leading coach, with the locomotive hauling the train on the return journey. Notice the sand box feeding the rear driving wheel to obviate slipping, and also the tool box beside the splasher of the leading driving wheel. The 'mushroom' above the side tank allowed air to escape when the tank was filled with water.

Laurence Waters

One of the most successful GWR designs was the 'Castle' class, developed from the much earlier 'Star' class. The former was introduced in 1923. In the early fifties 168 of these machines were in service, some being built post-war. 'Castles' were allocated to many Western Region depots. Here, No. 5034 *Corfe Castle*, an Old Oak Common engine, drifts into Paddington at the end of its journey on 7.5.55. Eight 'Castles' still survive, one of which is No. 4079 *Pendennis Castle*. This is now a long way from home, being at the Hammersley Iron Company's line in Australia, where it is regularly seen in action. No. 4073 *Caerphilly Castle* is in the Science Museum, London. The remaining six can be found at various preservation centres, several examples being in full working order and seen from time to time on BR.

E.H. Sawford

Summer Saturdays at Aberystwyth offered the prospect of trains travelling southwards to Carmarthen, narrow gauge services to Devil's Bridge and, of course, on the main route to Machynlleth and onwards to Shrewsbury. There was also a solitary named train which conveyed through coaches and a restaurant car to Paddington – the 'Cambrian Coast Express'. The only class of GWR locomotives with the 4–6–0 wheel arrangement allowed as far west as this in mid-Wales was the 'Manor', and Aberystwyth depot, a sub-shed of 89C (Machynlleth), certainly knew how to look after them. On 27.8.60 No. 7802 *Bradley Manor* looked spotless, with white-painted buffers and smokebox door handles to intensify the effect. On the dot of 9.45 a.m. this immaculate locomotive made a most impressive exit from the coastal resort at the head of chocolate and cream carriages bound for London. Today *Bradley Manor* is preserved on the Severn Valley Railway.

David Fereday Glenn

'Castle' class 4–6–0 No. 5038 *Morlais Castle* of Shrewsbury shed stands at its home station on 27.8.60 at the head of an Up express, probably for Paddington. The platform is a hive of activity, with baggage, luggage trolleys, people talking and others seeing friends off on their journeys, while spotters are also in evidence. The fireman looks back down the train, perhaps to see how close it is to departure time.

Maurice Dart

Although decried by their critics as showing no variety, to the trained observer former GWR engines possessed many differences. This photograph shows an example of one of the 'Grange' class 4–6–0s, No. 6833 *Calcot Grange*. It is away from home metals as the location is Clapham Junction in 1956, thus indicating a through working. To add to the variety, it is hauling ex-LMS coaches. Many locomotive men believed the 'Grange' was the epitome of a good mixed-traffic engine, capable of hauling all but the fastest and heaviest trains, yet without placing untoward demands upon its crew. Eighty were built from August 1936 onwards, but sadly none survived into preservation.

Kevin Robertson Collection/W. Gilburt

'Manor' class 4–6–0 No. 7828 *Odney Manor* of 89C (Machynlleth) heads the Down 'Cambrian Coast Express' at Shrewsbury on 11.9.63. *Odney Manor* is now preserved on the East Lancashire Railway. Notice the step below the smokebox door to assist the placing of a headboard, or lamp, on the top bracket. To the left of the locomotive is a kitchen car.

Laurence Waters Collection/D. Tuck

Ex-GWR 8750 class 0–6–0PT No. 9773 at Oxford on station pilot duty, on 28.8.63. Apart from shunting duties, these very versatile engines were used for working pick-up goods trains, local passenger duties, and sometimes even appeared on short-distance expresses. Having pannier tanks, rather than side tanks, allowed easy accessibility to the inside cylinders and motion. No. 9773 was withdrawn in December 1965.

Laurence Waters Collection/D. Tuck

Country Stations

Class J39/3 0–6–0 No. 64843 at Eyemouth, heading a train to Burnmouth Junction on the Berwick-upon-Tweed to Edinburgh main line. At the photographer's end of the station building is a trailer belonging to a mechanical horse, while on the right a coal lorry can be seen with L-plates. Note that the station has electric lights and that the platform is unusually wide. This view was taken in August 1959.

R.E. Toop

THE COUNTRY STATION was an important feature of a village, on a par with the church, school and public house. In the heyday of the postcard, *c.* 1910, the local post office would sell views of the village church and the station. The station-master was a man of standing and, if wise, he cultivated the friendship of his neighbours in order to win traffic for his railway company. He sought farmers and industrialists for freight, and the headmaster and vicar to win potential excursion traffic. A country station-master was in charge of a small empire. Circumstances varied, but generally he would have been in charge of quite a few people: at least one booking clerk; two porters (one on the early and one on the late turn); perhaps a lad porter; a goods porter; and two or three signalmen, depending on whether or not the box was open for twenty-four hours. Latterly the station might have had its own lorry, but more probably one based at a town station called as the need arose to deal with collections and deliveries. Staff were often imaginative and innovative, with ideas for making and distributing pocket local timetables and setting up attractive boards advertising excursions. But not all country stations had a large staff, and at some the station-master was also the porter, signalman, booking clerk, parcels clerk and every other office the station required.

Country stations situated in a well-farmed area tended to be no more than about 4 miles from each other, so that a horse and cart would not have to travel more than about 2 miles to reach a station.

Traffic at country stations varied according to local circumstances, but was principally coal (unless in a wood- or peat-burning area), animal foodstuffs, farm machinery, cattle, and supplies for shops. Outward traffic would be agricultural products, including live cattle.

The lighting of the station might be by oil, Tilley pressure lamp or gaslight, electricity being rare on country stations. A station garden would probably be maintained, while railwaymen often had lineside allotments to provide fresh vegetables, with ash from the locomotives being used to prevent attack from slugs.

A job on the railway usually offered better pay than on a farm and, until the Beeching era, was a job for life, providing the company's rules were kept. Being a railwayman was like being a member of a large family: surplus produce would be exchanged, newspapers and magazines left in compartments handed down the line, and the availability advertised of free offerings such as bean sticks, mushrooms and blackberries.

If the country station was in a holiday area, the yard might accommodate a camping coach or two during the summer months. Camping coaches were old vehicles adapted to provide cooking and sleeping facilities and could be hired for reasonable rates, a condition being that the occupants travelled to the coach by rail.

The country station signal-box was a magical place, with shining levers, not touched by hand but always with a duster so as not to mark them. The levers were colourful, being coded for the various signals and points they operated. On the shelf above the lever frame were bells and instruments which showed whether there was a train on the line, and if signal lamps out of the signalman's sight were alight. The floor usually sparkled and some particularly proud signalmen insisted that all visitors removed their footwear and donned slippers, or came in stockinged feet. Boxes on single lines had the added attraction of having a staff, token or tablet to be issued and collected from the fireman, giving authority to travel over the line. Usually exchange was by hand, but on some busy lines this was carried out by an ingenious apparatus which usually, but not invariably, worked. A lost tablet was serious matter, as it meant that no train could travel until it was either found or another method of train working instituted. The signals a box operated could be of a number of varieties: upper or lower quadrant; home or distant; on a single mast or gantry; on a tall post to be observed above a bridge, or underslung so as to be sighted below a structure.

Country stations were not quite as crazy as that featured in the film *Oh Mr Porter*, but amusing events occurred from time to time, such as when some white pigs ran amok amid tar barrels.

Ex-Caledonian Railway 72 class 4–4–0 No. 54495, deputizing for the usual class 5 4–6–0, arrives at Nairn with a Forres to Inverness local train in August 1959. The paintwork at the foot of the smokebox door appears to be burnt, suggesting that at some time the engine has been worked very hard; it was not unknown for the door to glow red-hot. The platform on the right is of an unusual width.

R.E. Toop

Before Nationalization, rival railways serving different termini met at Crianlarich, Perthshire. The Callander and Oban section of the LMS occupied the low-level station, while the West Highland line between Glasgow Queen Street and Fort William was administered by the LNER, which used the upper station. A short, single-track link was built between the two Crianlarich stations for interchange purposes, but had no regular use until a landslip closed the former LMS route via Balquidder in late 1965.

On 5.9.60 the 10.05 a.m. from Glasgow Queen Street forges out of Crianlarich Upper station behind a brace of class 5MT 4–6–0s bound for Fort William and Mallaig. BR Standard class 5 No. 73109 is coupled ahead of Stanier 'Black Five' No. 44996 for the 6 mile climb to Tyndrum, 940 ft above sea level, the heavy train including a restaurant car and observation coach.

David Fereday Glenn

Nestling amid the Westmorland hills, Tebay was a junction station complete with its own small locomotive depot, coded 12H. Engines based here were employed primarily on banking duties northward over Shap summit. In times past the shed also provided power for the difficult North Eastern Railway route through Ravenstonedale to Kirkby Stephen (East) and Barnard Castle.

On 15.8.61 a train of empty milk tanks is hustled on the main line through Tebay by 'Jubilee' class 4–6–0 No. 45596 *Bahamas*, the six-wheel wagons beating a wild tattoo over the points for the Kirkby Stephen branch, while a Fowler class 4 2–6–4T toys with some ballast trucks in the yard. *Bahamas* was one of the few members of the 'Jubilee' class to be equipped with a double chimney. She is now preserved on the Keighley and Worth Valley Railway.

David Fereday Glenn

'Jubilee' class 4–6–0 No. 45643 *Rodney*, of 5A (Crewe North), passes Beattock with a Down express on 12.8.58. The platform edge, instead of being delineated by a continuous white line, is marked by a more economic broken one. On the left the engine shed roof is receiving attention. The building housed bankers to assist trains up the 10 mile-long Beattock bank, which has an average gradient of about 1 in 75.

R.E. Toop

A spotter notes the number of class 6P5F 2–6–0 No. 42958 as it passes Abergele, Denbighshire, with a fitted freight on 13.8.63. This engine is a Stanier taper-boiler version of Hughes' parallel-boiler design. Only forty of the former were built, but 245 of the latter. Much of the design work of this Stanier 2–6–0 was carried over to his better-known class 5 mixed traffic and class 8F engines.

Abergele was the scene of a terrible disaster on 20.8.1867, when runaway wagons collided with the 'Irish Mail', spraying it with paraffin oil. The resulting inferno caused the deaths of thirty-two passengers in the leading coaches.

A typical London and North Western Railway signal-box is on the left. Note that the station has a public-address system.

R.E. Toop

In the course of its long history the railway has developed an ability to create memorable occasions. One such was on 15.9.63. The influence of Scottish locomotive designs during the late nineteenth and early twentieth centuries was immense, for men like Stroudley and Drummond, having made their mark north of the border, moved south to bring developments to companies that were to become constituents of the Southern Railway in 1923.

Depicted here is the famous Caledonian Railway Drummond 4–2–2 No. 123, brought down from Glasgow to London to work the final through excursion from the Metropolis to the Bluebell Railway, in tandem with the sole-surviving Drummond 'Greyhound' class T9 4–4–0, No. 120. At the end of a glorious late-summer day, the two Victorian engines began the return journey from Haywards Heath in double-traction to the acclaim of all present.

David Fereday Glenn

Watched by a photographer, ex-LMS rebuilt 'Royal Scot' class 4–6–0 No. 46134 *The Cheshire Regiment* passes Oxenholme with a Glasgow to Manchester express in June 1960.

Laurence Waters Collection/W. Turner

'Jubilee' class 4–6–0 No. 45638 *Zanzibar*, of 5A (Crewe North), stands at Windermere with an express to Euston in the summer of 1961. Note that the platform lamps are still lit by gas.

Laurence Waters Collection/W. Turner

'Jubilee' class 4–6–0 No. 45627 *Sierra Leone* stands at Windermere with a train of empty coaching stock, while on the right is Fairburn class 4 2–6–4T No. 42299 of 24L (Carnforth) with the 2.00 p.m. stopping train to Kendal and Oxenholme. Notice the oval buffers used on some LMS locomotives. With slight modifications, this design of 2–6–4T was adopted by BR as a Standard class. The photograph was taken on 12.8.63.

R.E. Toop

Class 5 4–6–0 No. 44892 runs through Oxenholme with a Down ballast train in June 1960. The hazy exhaust reveals that the fireman is putting on coal, Oxenholme being on a rising gradient of 1 in 178 and near the start of the 24 mile-long gradient to Shap, only broken by five level miles between Grayrigg and Tebay. This severe gradient, of consequence in steam days, is hardly noticed by today's electrics.

Laurence Waters Collection/W. Turner

Resting at Llandudno Junction station is 'Princess Coronation' class 4–6–2 No. 46238 *City of Carlisle*. These large ex-LMS Pacifics were transferred to the Crewe–Holyhead line from the West Coast main line following electrification of the Euston route, the diagonal cab-side stripe denoting that the locomotive was banned from operating under the wires beyond Crewe.

This engine was photographed at the west end of Llandudno Junction station, where a water tank was situated to supply Down locomotives. Just beyond the tank was the tallest semaphore signal on the North Wales Coast line. This signal had to be tall to ensure visibility well beyond the eastern end of the station. Semaphores have long since been replaced by three-aspect colour light signals.

Mike Hitches Collection/Peter Owen

One of the most graceful 4–4–0 designs introduced to Britain, the D40 class, made its first appearance in 1899 as a Pickersgill design for the Great North of Scotland Railway. In 1920 a further batch of eight was built, these being superheated locomotives introduced by T. Heywood, locomotive superintendent of the Great North of Scotland Railway from 1914 until 1922. All the later locomotives were named, one of which, No. 62277 *Gordon Highlander*, is preserved.

The engine in this photograph taken at Keith, No. 62264, was completed by Neilson and Company in October 1899. When photographed on 24.8.55 it was acting as carriage pilot. Despite its smart appearance it had just two months left in service before it was withdrawn. In 1954 Keith had an allocation of nineteen engines, twelve of these belonging to the D40 class.

E.H. Sawford

Class K3 2–6–0 No. 61928 of 64A (St Margaret's, Edinburgh) passes Longtown with a freight on the Edinburgh to Carlisle line on 18.8.59. Engines of this class had a massive boiler and a squat chimney.

R.E. Toop

Class B1 4–6–0 No. 61397 with a stopping train at Elgin, Morayshire, on 14.8.59. This general purpose-type engine was suitable for all but the heaviest trains, and over four hundred were constructed. They ranged over most of the LNER system, and in the days of Nationalization ventured as far as the North Wales coast and down to Weston-super-Mare.

R.E. Toop

B1 class 4–6–0 locomotives were certainly not strangers to the East Coast main line south of Peterborough during the fifties. Most of their duties involved local passenger, excursions, parcels and goods traffic, including fast fish trains which were still a daily feature at the time.

Only one regular express train was worked by a B1, although these engines were not unknown on such duties when they took over from a failed locomotive. The regular express turn was the King's Cross to Cleethorpes service, always worked by an Immingham depot B1. This nine-coach train was booked with a fast timing in both directions on the main line.

Several B1s were allocated to Immingham, and most appeared on this service. They were maintained in good mechanical and external condition, as can be clearly seen from this photograph. Here, an immaculate No. 61082 blasts away from Huntingdon, the first stop on its homeward journey, in the early evening of 27.7.57.

When the 'Britannias' were replaced on the East Anglian services, several were transferred to Immingham, taking over this Cleethorpes duty from the B1s.

E.H. Sawford

Typical of the condition of BR's steam locomotive fleet as it was speedily replaced by modern traction, is this view of dilapidated-looking BR Standard 'Britannia' Pacific No. 70023 *Rising Star*, shorn of nameplates and smokebox numberplate, standing at the head of a Holyhead-bound train at Llandudno Junction in the early 1960s.

These engines were first introduced on the North Wales Coast line in 1954 to replace ex-LMS 'Royal Scot' class 4–6–0s on the 'Irish Mail', running between Euston and the packet port for Ireland. Numbers used increased considerably in the declining years of steam operation and *Britannia* herself could sometimes be seen hauling trains between Crewe and Holyhead. These glorious days were partly re-created during the summer of 1992 when No. 70000 *Britannia* worked a few steam excursions along the North Wales Coast line.

Mike Hitches Collection / Gwyn Roberts

BR Standard class 5 4–6–0 No. 73166 of 83D (Laira) at Dinton, west of Salisbury, with an Up goods train. The high running plate gives easy access for oiling. Unlike the Western Region, the Southern Region used discs, rather than lamps, during daylight. Note the white edge to the platform, helping passengers to avoid falling onto the permanent way. In this view the rail is of the flat-bottomed type which BR introduced to most main lines in the fifties and sixties. The photograph was taken on 8.4.64.

Colin G. Maggs

BR Standard class 4 2–6–0 No. 76028 of 71A (Eastleigh) at Collingbourne Kingston Halt, heading the 1.52 p.m. Cheltenham to Southampton service. The 'SC' below the shed plate indicates that the engine has a self-cleaning smokebox, a device which avoided the labour and unpleasantness of shovelling out ash. The line was the former Midland and South Western Junction Railway, most of which was closed when the passenger train service was withdrawn in September 1961, the only sections open today being from Andover to Ludgershall, and a short length relaid by the Swindon and Cricklade Railway. This view was taken 17.4.61.

Colin G. Maggs

BR Standard class 4 4–6–0s Nos 75020 and 75021 head a train for Shrewsbury. Machynlleth has a substantial station building. The safety valves of No. 75020 are blowing off, while the fireman tops up the tender with water, on 11.9.63.

Laurence Waters Collection/D. Tuck

BR Standard class 4 4–6–0 No. 75002 leaves Barmouth in 1964. One disadvantage of a steam engine was that its exhaust could conceal the view, this photograph being a good example. Steam and smoke drifted down, hiding the scenery from passengers, and more seriously, making signal-sighting more difficult for the footplate crew.

Colin G. Maggs Collection/W.H. Harbor

The arctic conditions prevailing at the beginning of 1963 caused only minor disruption to the Hayling Island branch. Minus the familiar spark-arrester on the chimney, Stroudley class A1X 0–6–0T No. 32661 drifted into North Hayling Halt with the 11.35 a.m. from Havant on 8.1.63 – no one alighted and no one boarded. The 'Terriers' had been introduced for light passenger traffic on the London, Brighton and South Coast Railway in 1872. They first became associated with the Hayling line in the 1890s and remained the standard motive power until the branch was closed to all traffic in November 1963.

David Fereday Glenn

M7 class 0–4–4T No. 30254 shunting at Barnstaple in 1963. As the driving wheels were towards the front, this design gave plenty of room for a firebox. Notice that the bunker has been modified to enable a larger supply of coal to be carried. The front of the splasher forms a sand box.

Laurence Waters

Ex-London and South Western Railway 02 class 0–4–4T No. W18 *Ningwood* standing at Ryde Pierhead with a train for Shanklin in June 1961. The train is literally above the sea, which is immediately below the empty spaces. Engines on the Isle of Wight did not carry a smokebox numberplate, but had it painted on the buffer beam in the traditional fashion. The 02s were older, lighter and less powerful than the M7 class.

Laurence Waters Collection/W. Turner

The former South Eastern and Chatham Railway's cross-country route between Reading, Guildford, Redhill and Tonbridge witnessed a wide variety of motive power in the final years of steam. As well as examples from each of the Southern Railway's pre-Grouping constituents, BR Standard designs, together with a few GWR mixed-traffic locomotives and Bulleid's unique 'Austerity' class Q1 0–6–0s, appeared regularly on the line. While their usual role was hauling freight, on 7.12.61 No. 33025 was entrusted with the 9.45 a.m. Reading to Redhill service and is seen here bustling out of Shalford station before the winter sunshine has had a chance to melt the overnight frost.

David Fereday Glenn

The first station at Petworth opened in 1859 as the terminus of a branch line from Pulborough; not until 1866 was the line extended to Midhurst. A larger station was opened at Petworth in 1892, about 2 miles south of the town itself.

With closure of the signal-box at Petworth, following the withdrawal of passenger services, a ground frame was installed which was released using the single-line token. On 4.7.60 a member of the train crew operates this frame to allow shunting to take place in the yard.

Class E4 0–6–2T No. 32470 of 75D (Horsham) occupies the platform with the 12.30 p.m. pick-up goods from Midhurst, safety valves lifting in anticipation of further activity. Freight traffic was withdrawn in May 1966.

David Fereday Glenn

The footplate crew dampen down the tender coal-space before 'Merchant Navy' class Pacific No. 35007 *Aberdeen Commonwealth* departs from Weymouth with the 1730 to Waterloo on 15.6.67. With the nameplates removed for safekeeping and the lenses for the middle set of electric route lamps missing, the locomotive is nonetheless in a relatively clean condition for the last few weeks of steam, although there is evidence of burning on the smokebox door. No. 35007 attained a speed of 98 mph on the same service as that photographed here on 6.7.67, just three days before the end of Southern steam.

A.J. Fry Collection

Class 2251 0–6–0 No. 2247 of 86A (Newport, Ebbw Junction) heads the 2.05 p.m. Brecon to Newport stopping train at Bargoed on 15.9.62. Dieselization has already come to the Valleys, as a plate indicating the stopping point for a six-car DMU can be seen near the foot of the water tower. No. 2247 was withdrawn in February 1964.

R.E. Toop

The white-painted buffers and smokebox door straps contrast with the empty nameplate holder on rebuilt 'West Country' class Pacific No. 34013 *Okehampton*, seen here at Radipole Halt with the 1445 'fruit' from Weymouth to Westbury on 15.6.67. Radipole, the final stop before Weymouth, opened in 1905 and its examples of the classic GWR pagoda-style waiting shelters can be seen here. The axe fell on Southern steam three weeks after this photograph was taken, and the halt closed some seventeen years later in February 1984.

A.J. Fry Collection

On the Gloucester to Swindon line, a number of halts were built between Stonehouse and Chalford at intervals of approximately three-quarters of a mile to serve local communities. Steam railmotors or autotrains provided the service until replaced by buses in November 1964. Collett 0–4–2T No. 1472, built in 1936, was in charge of the single autocar forming the 8.42 a.m. from Stonehouse (Burdett Road) on 31.10.62, bustling away from the staggered platforms of Brimscombe Bridge Halt towards the Golden Valley. Originally No. 4872, it became No. 1472 after the Second World War. Unlike most of the class, it was never equipped with top-feed apparatus, but gained lined green livery in its final years, being withdrawn on cessation of the Chalford auto services in November 1964.

David Fereday Glenn

Class 5101 2–6–2T No. 4110 at Wellington (Salop) with a stopping train to Much Wenlock. A DMU to Birmingham and Lapworth stands on the right, with motor second three-car Swindon 'Cross-Country' unit No. W50656 leading. Notice the gas lamps and the circular flowerbed. The date is 21.8.59. No. 4110 is preserved at Southall Railway Centre.

R.E. Toop

Class 2251 0–6–0 No. 2247 of 86A (Newport, Ebbw Junction) with the 2.05 p.m. Brecon to Newport stopping train, in the bay platform at Brecon on 17.9.62. The impressive station building, reminiscent of a country mansion, was the headquarters of the Brecon and Merthyr Railway. Sister engine No. 2298 has obeyed the notice 'All engines must stop before going on this turntable'. Note the loading gauge on the turntable road.

R.E. Toop

'County' class 4–6–0 No. 1008 *County of Cardigan* of 83D (Laira) departs from St Austell in the evening sun of 1.6.60 with the 1.30 p.m. ex-Paddington to Penzance express. This view from the signal-box shows vans in the Up sidings and a solitary brake van in the Down sidings adjacent to a collection of Western National buses parked outside their depot which was originally the GWR goods shed. These sidings have now all been removed. *County of Cardigan* was withdrawn in October 1963.

Maurice Dart

'Grange' class 4–6–0 No. 6848 *Toddington Grange* of 88D (Merthyr) at Yatton, Avon, with a Down stopping train in June 1956. The rare underslung signals, almost centrally pivoted, were designed so that they were not obscured by the signal gantry sited above the coaches. Chained to the post is a ladder for placing on the crossbar between the two signals in order to reach the lamps so that they could be cleaned, trimmed and re-filled.

Yatton station is still open, but is no longer the junction for the Clevedon and Cheddar Valley branches, these having been closed during the Beeching era. *Toddington Grange* was withdrawn in December 1965.

Colin G. Maggs Collection / W.H. Harbor

Class 16XX 0–6–0PT No. 1626 of 83E (St Blazey) brings a rake of brake vans into Fowey station past the signal-box on a wet Cornish morning. These were to form a special train organized by the Plymouth Railway Circle which covered the line through Pinnock tunnel to St Blazey, up Luxulyan bank to Goonbarrow Junction and also traversed the branch to Gunheath and Carbean. It ended, almost 1¾ hours behind schedule, with an optional visit to St Blazey shed. Members of the party taking advantage of this detrained at the closed St Blazey station and walked over foot crossings to the shed. The section of line depicted in the photograph of 22.4.61 is now a 'haul road' for lorries carrying china clay to Fowey docks.

Maurice Dart

Framed by a GWR tubular signal gantry is 5101 class 2–6–2T No. 4103 as it approaches Stroud from Swindon on a freight duty in August 1964. Today there are no signals at Stroud, the goods yard has gone and so too has the timber signal-box. However, Brunel's Cotswold stone goods shed still stands and is a Listed building. No. 4103 was withdrawn the month after this picture was taken.

Alan Postlethwaite

A splendid study of the double-chimney 'Castle' class No. 5057 *Earl Waldegrave* of 81A (Old Oak Common) at Newbury Racecourse station on 27.7.63. It is in good external condition, yet it is sad to think that it was withdrawn in March 1964, less than a year later.

Laurence Waters Collection / D. Tuck

'Manor' class 4–6–0 No. 7828 *Odney Manor* of 89C (Machynlleth) at its home station with the Down 'Cambrian Coast Express' on 11.9.63. The footplateman is correctly looking out of the cab to make sure that all is well with the train. To the right is a 'mushroom'-type water tank and water crane. *Odney Manor* is preserved by the East Lancashire Railway.

Laurence Waters Collection/D. Tuck

Locomotives at Home

A surprise visitor at Barry shed was 56XX class 0–6–2T No. 5612 of 87F (Llanelly). The train identification number carried on the smokebox door conceals the locomotive's identity, but reveals that it had worked an excursion from Llanelly to Barry Island and was being prepared at Barry shed to work the return train in the early evening.

The line of locomotives on the left were all tank engines shedded at Barry, and include 57XX class 0–6–0PT No. 7764, 94XX class 0–6–0PT No. 9425, and 8750 and 56XX class engines. The photograph was taken on 26.6.60.

Maurice Dart

RAILWAY ENTHUSIASTS FOUND STEAM locomotive sheds exciting. There was the smell of steam and burning coal, and the engines towering above you, with all but the very smallest dock shunter appearing so much larger when you were actually beside it. There was the smoky, gloomy atmosphere, for the lighting in most sheds was poor, and there was the excitement of discovering an unusual class of engine, or one from a remote shed. Various activities would be going on: cleaning paintwork; lighting or dropping fires; ash disposal; boiler washout; filling up with coal and water. At a large shed it was also common to see a live engine moving a dead one. If there was no coaling tower, wagons had to be shunted up a ramp to the coaling platform. This was an interesting event to watch, as the weight, coupled with the steep gradient, meant slipping was almost inevitable.

Turntables were another source of interest, with a driver getting his engine well-balanced in order to make the manual turning easier, though some very large sheds had a table turned by a motor worked off the vacuum pipe.

Although magical places for the enthusiast, sheds were not quite so delightful for those who had to work there. One fireman wrote of the difficulties experienced removing clinker from the firebox of an ex-LMS Fowler 2–6–4T with a 10 ft-long shovel:

It was a difficult task manoeuvring a shovel full of clinker out of that box to deposit the clinker on the ash heap, the handle protruding through the opening on the fireman's side of the cab and the blade out the driver's side. The fact that the handle grew very hot, eventually glowing red hot, only added to my difficulties. They were most awkward engines to dispose of, in fact, contrary to regulations, it wasn't uncommon for a couple of firebars to be taken up, the clinker shovelled through the ashpan, the driver getting underneath and raking it out. He used a hose pipe to spray water into the ashpan so that the choking, hot dust was immediately damped down and cooled, enabling him to rake it out immediately like wet, slaggy mud, leaving a perfectly clean ashpan and a perfectly clean grate. So far the work had been tolerably easy and pleasant, but the task of putting the set of bars back in was a little bit tricky. Those taken out were from the middle section of the box. To remove them was easy – you simply took an iron with little twin hooks on, dropped it down over a bar, and as the end of the bar was lugged, it was a simple matter to place the hooks under the lugs, lift, pull and you'd got one out. You pulled it straight out of the box on to the footplate red hot, leaving it there to cool.

To put a firebar in, you utilized a bar with a small L-shaped end like a little pricker. You placed a firebar in the box on its side, and manoeuvred it into the exact position you wanted – this operation being carried out at a distance of about seven feet from the person doing it – suddenly tipped it so it dropped into place. The first bar in, you pushed it up tight against those left in; the second bar was put in and you pushed that up. Now came the problem. The third was always a tight fit. You'd already cleaned the rack where they rested so that it was free of ash and clinker and would allow the bars to fall in flat. Once the third bar was in, you made

it go up and down so that it acted as a hammer eight feet away from you, making sure it sat flat and not proud.

If an engine was going into traffic within three or four hours of arriving at the shed, the approved method of fire-cleaning was this:

The dampers were shut, the engine stood over a pit with perhaps 140 to 150 lb of steam, that is 50 lb below normal, and a boiler full of water. A bent dart, which was an iron with an arrow-shaped head, was pushed under the door, the clinker pushed forward clearing the back of the box of everything. Then, using a clinker shovel, any clean fire was taken off the top of the clinker and by withdrawing the shovel and turning it over, the clean fire dropped under the firehole door, perhaps half a dozen to a dozen shovelfuls. Next, a couple of dozen lumps of fresh coal were put on top to catch alight. All the clinker was now at the front of the box. I then got a straight dart and ran it down the remaining bars to break the clinker which sometimes formed plates an inch deep and three to four feet in diameter. If possible, this was broken up into a convenient size for disposal, but sometimes it was very hard and difficult to break. Then, using the clinker shovel, the rest of the box was cleared out completely, leaving the coal burning under the door.

The same fireman recorded the job of lighting a fire:

When steam raiser knew it was time to light an engine up, in other words, about eight hours before she was wanted for traffic, he got aboard and threw in about seven to eight hundredweight of coal, leaving a space in the middle under the firehole door. Then he added half-a-dozen firelighters and another dozen coal lumps on top; left the damper open, shut the firebox door and left her to her own devices. Black smoke poured out of cracks round the door and blackened everything in the cab, you could always tell by its appearance when an engine had been lit up. One thing that had to be remembered was to test the injectors before you'd built a fire up to any extent, because if they didn't work, you were the one who had to throw the fire out again.

It was not unknown for engines to collide within the confines of the shed yard, one such incident occurring at Derby. Driver Frank Kerton and Fireman Bill Bagnall were taking 4–4–0 Compound No. 1027 for disposal when, to use Bill's words:

It was a foggy morning as we entered the yard and we had to look out for engines in front of us. I set the road for the Ash Pit and called to Frank, 'Alright, come ahead.' As No. 1027 started, I heard the dull rumbling of a moving engine coming towards us from the shed area and called to Frank, 'Whoa, set back.' We had the right of way, as any driver coming off the shed in that direction was expected to send his fireman forward to ensure that no engine was coming on the shed. We were over the points by the length of the bogie when out of the fog came a 'Crab' 2–6–0 and crashed into our engine. It knocked us off the road and bedded its buffer plank into us by the low pressure cylinder.

I went to the footplate and asked the driver what he thought he was doing. Just then his fireman, hearing the collision, came running up and shouted, 'That's what you get for running about in the fog without a mate.'

At the ensuing enquiry, when Chief Inspector Fellows was unsure which driver to believe, I said, 'A look at the buffer beams will surely indicate who was at fault. Our buffer beam is intact, but the 130XX's left-hand buffer is embedded in the region of our right-hand low pressure cylinder.' Fellows thought for a moment, obviously putting his mind to the geography of Derby shed. Then he shut up his book, gathered his papers and said, 'I'm satisfied now what had happened. You and your driver are in the clear.'

There were other occasional shed disasters, such as leaving a regulator slightly open on a dead engine, so that when steam was raised the engine moved off – perhaps into a turntable pit. Steam pressure, or lack of it, also caused a problem when there was enough steam to move but not enough to work the brakes.

A fine line of locomotives on the afternoon of Easter Sunday, 12.4.60, at Radyr shed, situated north of Cardiff where the main Taff Vale line met the Penarth Railway at Penarth Branch Junction. In GWR and early BR days Radyr shed was regarded as a sub-shed of Cardiff Cathays, but nevertheless had its own GWR shed code of 'RYR'. In the BR era it became 88A. Its allocation numbered about twenty-eight locomotives, but when Cathays closed to steam in 1961 Radyr gained all its engines.

Locomotives in this picture are:

5101 class 2–6–2T: No. 4160 (Radyr)

56XX class 0–6–2T: No. 6608 (Radyr); No. 6648 (Radyr); No. 6626 (Radyr); No. 5618 (Radyr); No. 6682 (Radyr); No. 5600 (88F, signifying either Treherbert or Ferndale).

94XX class 0–6–0PT: No. 3409, No. 8470 and No. 3402 (all of Radyr).

43XX class 2–6–0: No. 6377 (Carmarthen).

The latter engine was most surprising, as tender engines rarely visited Radyr. It was on its way to Caerphilly Works. No. 4160 is now preserved on the West Somerset Railway.

Maurice Dart

Sunlight filters through the roof of Scarborough straight shed on to D49/2 'Hunt' class 4–4–0 No. 62739 *The Badsworth* in its home depot on 14.8.60. Note the fox depicted above the locomotive's nameplate. Diesels were in evidence here and within a few months this engine was withdrawn. The roundhouse at the other end of the shed yard was used only for storing withdrawn steam locomotives. The shed closed completely on 22.4.63 and was demolished.

Maurice Dart

Over the years the small repair shop at New England, Peterborough depot has attended to many locomotives, both from the depot's own allocation and to visitors. Time was running out when this photograph was taken on 6.12.64, as New England was due to close to steam in just three weeks. In the previous few years several A3 class Pacifics were allocated to the depot, including No. 60062 *Minoru*, which is seen here receiving attention. This engine was in its final form, with German-type smoke deflectors and double chimney. Like all remaining examples at that time, it was in a very shabby condition.

E.H. Sawford

BR Standard class 3MT 2–6–2T No. 82005 at Machynlleth shed on 11.9.63. Note the bunker piled high with coal and the curved pipe attached to the rear of the cab which could spray water on the fuel to lay the dust – a particularly useful feature when running bunker-first. The upper part of the bunker is inset to allow good visibility when running bunker-first. Below the engine is an inspection pit. Note that this modern engine is designed for easy maintenance, with many of its moving parts easily accessible.

Laurence Waters Collection / D. Tuck

Crewe Works was responsible for constructing the BR Standard Pacifics, introduced in 1951 with No. 70000 *Britannia*. Here, the second member of the class, No. 70001 *Lord Hurcomb*, of 2J (Aston), is seen outside Crewe North shed on 22.3.65, very near the end of its life, after only fourteen years in service. The old locomotive sheds, along with most of the works, have now disappeared.

Mike Hitches Collection / Terry Roberts

Class 45XX 2–6–2T No. 5552 of Truro simmers in the sidings between the coaling plant and the main line at Truro shed on 12.7.58, a day of torrential rain. This locomotive was withdrawn from Truro in October 1960 and languished at Woodham Brothers' scrapyard at Barry until rescued and taken to Bodmin, where it is undergoing restoration. In the background can be seen carriage sidings and the end of the goods yard adjacent to Truro passenger station.

Maurice Dart

Ex-Cardiff Railway 0–4–0ST No. 1338 of Taunton shed at the rear of the small sub-shed at Bridgwater on 22.3.59. This diminutive engine was originally Cardiff Railway No. 5, built by Messrs Kitson in 1898. After leaving Cardiff it worked at Swansea East dock then Bridgwater, before returning to Swansea East dock, from where it was withdrawn in September 1963. While at Bridgwater the engine shunted the sidings at Dunball wharf. Its buffers are an unusual shape. No. 1338 was first preserved at Bleadon and Uphill station near Weston-super-Mare, but is now at Didcot Steam Centre.

Maurice Dart

Only five of these sturdy 1361 class 0–6–0STs were built, the design being introduced for dock shunting in 1910.

Of the five examples, four were usually allocated to 83D, Laira depot, Plymouth, while the fifth, No. 1362, was allocated to Taunton during the mid-fifties. The Plymouth engines were principally used in the docks. This view shows No. 1361 having its saddle tank filled before another spell of duty. All five lasted until the sixties. In 1934 Collett introduced six engines of the 1366 class, which was really a pannier tank version of the 1361 class.

The water crane, with its stove, is a principal feature of this photograph. The man controls the on/off cock. In the background can be seen heavy lifting gear, required when repairing locomotives.

E.H. Sawford

Class 57XX 0–6–0PT No. 9648 of 88H (Tondu) at its home shed on 22.6.63. Note that the shed plate has been inverted but still reads the correct letter and number. Ash from the smokebox lies on the front buffer beam. No. 9648 was withdrawn in July 1964.

Laurence Waters

Class 56XX 0–6–2T No. 6697 of Croes Newydd shed shunts wagons of coal up the ramp to the coal stage at its home shed on a very wintry day, despite the date, 15.4.66. By this time the shed had come under the aegis of the London Midland Region of BR, and in addition to many withdrawn ex-GWR pannier tank engines in the yard, the roundhouse hosted 'Black Fives' and 8Fs. The shedman supervising the shunting stands in a huddled, shivering stance with his hands concealed for warmth, as it was actually snowing when the photograph was taken. No. 6697 has lost its BR smokebox numberplate and carries a GWR-type number painted on its buffer beam, having recently worked an enthusiasts' railtour. No. 6697 is now preserved at Didcot Steam Centre. Croes Newydd shed closed on 5.6.67 and was later demolished.

Maurice Dart

Dowlais Cae Harris shed on Sunday morning 19.8.62, showing two of the five occupants, all of which were 56XX class 0–6–2Ts. No. 5660 stands in front of No. 5671, 88D signifying the parent shed of Merthyr, which in BR days shared a common shed code with Rhymney, Cae Harris and Dowlais Central. In GWR days these sheds each had an individual shed code.

The position of the inside cylinders can be seen below the smokebox. The 56XX class was the largest GWR tank engine to have inside cylinders.

Maurice Dart

Class 57XX 0–6–0PT No. 7772 at St Philip's Marsh shed, Bristol, on 12.4.61. The locomotive was withdrawn in November that year. This photograph epitomizes the last days of steam – dirty engine, murky surroundings – though admittedly it was taken at 8.05 a.m. It was easy for Fireman Hathaway to stand on the flat top of the pannier tank to remove the leather bag from the tank filler. He would have been assisted by his driver swinging the arm of the water crane by means of the chain. The shed was modern enough to have electric light. Bristol had two ex-GWR sheds: St Philip's Marsh for goods engines, and Bath Road for those on passenger duties.

Colin G. Maggs

Compared with the numerous two cylinder 2–6–0 engines of the N and U classes, only twenty-six three-cylinder N1 and U1 examples existed, a number of these being rebuilds from earlier types. The three-cylinder design was easily identified by the vertical drop at the end of the running plate, depicted to advantage on class U1 No. 31901 at Reading South in June 1953. The main Western Region line to the West of England can be seen on the embankment to the right.

Kevin Robertson Collection/J.R. Fairman

Within the Home Counties and central southern England, severe disruption by snow is fortunately rare, though there have been some notable exceptions, such as 1947 and 1963. In preparation for such conditions, it was the practice for many years to adapt an engine at Eastleigh as a snowplough, this remaining in readiness throughout the winter. In 1963 this task fell to former 700 class 0–6–0 No. 30316, seen here outside the shed on 2.3.63.

Kevin Robertson Collection/J.R. Fairman

Fresh from overhaul at the neighbouring works, No. 30757 *Earl of Mount Edgecombe* poses in May 1949 alongside the office block at Eastleigh running shed, prior to returning to its more usual Devon haunts. It was unusual for a tank engine running on the British mainland to be named. No. 30757, together with a sister, were the two survivors of locomotives formerly owned by the Plymouth, Devonport and South Western Junction Railway.

From the open doorway on the left, countless locomen would enter or emerge between duties, some ignoring the presence of a youthful spotter, while others, perhaps after spending a day on an ill-steaming engine, would utter a sharp rebuke. The building also served as a dormitory for visiting locomotive crews, although how much sleep was possible so close to a busy locomotive shed is best left to the imagination.

Kevin Robertson Collection/W. Gilburt

Minus any vestige of ownership, 'Terrier' 0–6–0T No. 32662 stands at Fratton, Portsmouth in May 1950. Along with the equally diminutive P class engines, these were some of the smallest engines operating on the SR. Despite their small size – particularly apparent when standing alongside another engine or passenger coach – the class survived to work a number of lines over which larger engines were not permitted. With the advantage of character, simplicity, economy and lightness of weight, they are ideal machines for working lightly-loaded preserved lines and no less than ten survive. One was actually used as a public house sign until rescued for further railway use on the Isle of Wight!

Kevin Robertson Collection/W. Gilburt

An immaculate 'Schools' class 4–4–0 just ex-Ashford Works. No. 30905 *Tonbridge*, of Nine Elms, stands in the yard at Ashford shed on 1.9.58, awaiting a running-in turn. These handsome locomotives were the most powerful 4–4–0s in Great Britain. Designed by Maunsell, this particular engine was built in 1930 and withdrawn in 1961.

Maurice Dart

B4 class 0–4–0T No. 30102 of 72D (Plymouth Friary) in its shed yard with a vintage piece of rolling stock on 19.10.57. These little locomotives appeared quite impressive and businesslike with their outside cylinders and were designed for shunting at the company's docks at Southampton and Plymouth. Those at Friary shed worked traffic to North Quay (Sutton Harbour), the Cattewater branch and the siding to Bailey's timber wharf at Oreston, branching from the line to Turnchapel. Friary shed staff referred to these engines as 'Bugs'. The spark arrester on the chimney was a precaution when working timber wagons. Due to their antiquated appearance and their class, some Plymouth enthusiasts called them 'Befores'! They were replaced by 204 hp diesels. No. 30102 is now preserved at Bressingham Gardens Steam Museum, where it has been given its old name of *Granville*.

Maurice Dart

M7 class 0–4–4T No. 30667 of Exmouth Junction stands outside its home shed on a sunny Sunday afternoon, 7.4.63. In March 1961 the short-framed, non-motor-fitted No. 30667 was given a new lease of life with long frames and motor-train gear from No. 30128, withdrawn two months earlier. (Short-framed engines of this class had insufficient space for the air reservoir to be fitted ahead of the cylinders.) No. 30667 was finally withdrawn in May 1964.

Here, the photographer's friend and fellow enthusiast, Mike Daly, standing near the locomotive's bunker, was puzzling over why No. 30667 had a frame 1 ft 2¾ in longer than it was supposed to!

Maurice Dart

Three veteran Beattie 2–4–0WTs working the Wenford Bridge mineral line in north Cornwall were a Mecca for enthusiasts during the fifties. Introduced in 1874, these three examples outlived their eight-three classmates by more than half a century. Over the years they were rebuilt on several occasions: first by Adams, then by Urie, and finally by Maunsell. The SR classified them as the 0298 class. There was very little difference between the individual engines, the one exception being No. 30586, which was built up over the leading driving wheel splasher. Two survive in preservation, the one cut up being No. 30586, photographed here at Wadebridge on 5.9.56. It was withdrawn in December 1962 after covering 1,324,050 miles. The usual duty roster was for one locomotive to work the branch, another to shunt at Wadebridge, while the third was on stand-by or receiving maintenance.

E.H. Sawford

Rebuilt 'West Country' class Pacific No. 34100 *Appledore* awaiting its next duty at Salisbury shed in November 1966.

Rebuilding these Pacifics was controversial, and some of the changes are visible here. The shaft of the reverser can be seen on the side of the firebox from the cab to the running plate. Below the cab is the Stone's turbo-generator, supplying electrical power for the engine and tender route lamps, cab lighting, and sockets for the inspection lamps located below the running plate.

A.J. Fry Collection

Guildford shed was one of the last centres of steam. Here rebuilt 'West Country' class No. 34018 *Axminster*, in grimy condition and with missing number and name plates, waits to leave with a stores train to Woking on the last day of Southern steam, 9.7.67, from where it ran light engine to Salisbury. (A photograph of the locomotive en route to the scrapyard appears on page 142.)

Visible below the smokebox door is the Nife battery holder for the Automatic Warning System. On the running plate are sand boxes for the front and middle sets of driving wheels, and set between them are two Wakefield mechanical lubricators. The size of the nameplate is emphasized by the nameplate-holder behind the centre sand box filler.

A.J. Fry Collection

Often neglected by the enthusiast and photographer were the massive servicing facilities necessary to satisfy the voracious appetite of the steam engine. Here, Banbury coaling stage plays host to a line of three engines, led by class 5 4–6–0 No. 45493. Banbury was a former GWR shed and as such discharged Welsh coal which, being soft in texture, was unsuitable for mechanical handling. In consequence, manual labour had to be used, coal wagons being emptied by shovel into tubs ready to be tipped into the waiting tender. By the date this photograph was taken, 3.1.66, the labours of the coalmen were rapidly drawing to a close.

Kevin Robertson Collection/J.R. Fairman

The aftermath of a locomotive being engulfed in flames following its collision with a loaded petrol train at Didcot North in August 1964. The impact and fire occurred almost directly below a metal foot-bridge spanning the tracks, and this buckled in the severe heat. The high temperature caused the running plate of class 8F 2–8–0 No. 48734 to distort and, not surprisingly, following its removal to the nearby Didcot steam shed, the locomotive was condemned.

Kevin Robertson Collection/J.R. Fairman

Many freight engines enjoyed a lengthy life. One such type was the London and North Western Railway 'Super D' class 0–8–0. These engines were a development of the 0–6–0, the extra length allowing a larger boiler and firebox, yet still making all the driving wheels available for adhesion. Here at Bletchley in the summer of 1962 is a line-up of five withdrawn engines.

Laurence Waters Collection/W. Turner

The attractive Fowler-designed Somerset and Dorset Joint Railway 2–8–0s made their debut in 1914, six being built, with five more following in 1925. All were taken into LMS stock in 1930. In 1953 the entire class was allocated to Bath depot and usually at least two or three examples would be present there during the day. At this date Bath was a Southern Region MPD with the 71G shed code. Depicted is No. 53807, one of the later engines, in steam and standing on the coaling stage road. Coal roads were deliberately designed to be on a gradient, so that empty wagons could be run from the coaling stage by gravity and replaced by full wagons. Two members of the 1925 batch survive in preservation.

E.H. Sawford

The crew of class 3F 0–6–0 No. 43183 of 20D (Normanton) make a final check before taking it from its home shed on 13.5.56., with coal piled high in the tender.

Many class 3F 0–6–0s were still in service during the fifties. No. 43183 was an example of the eleven which had been rebuilt from an 1885 Midland Railway design, these particular engines having 4 ft 11 in diameter wheels instead of the more common 5 ft 3 ins.

Throughout the London Midland Region many classes of 0–6–0 tender engines were to be found, Midland designs alone numbering well over a thousand. Additionally, there were examples of Lancashire and Yorkshire, and London and North Western engines with the same wheel arrangement.

E.H. Sawford

An unexpected guest at Neath shed on 4.8.64 was the diminutive class 0F 0–4–0ST No. 51218. Christened by some wag 'Flying Magot' (*sic*), the 21 ton locomotive had been built at Horwich for the Lancashire and Yorkshire Railway in 1901. Note that instead of the usual spring buffers, it has solid wooden blocks. By the early 1960s it had ventured as far south as Bristol, Barrow Road depot, before moving into Wales to assist with light shunting in the Swansea area. As the last example of its class in service with BR, it has found a home on the Keighley and Worth Valley Railway, in company with fellow member of its class No. 11243.

David Fereday Glenn

Class 8F 2–8–0 No. 48214 of 16D (Nottingham) at Bletchley MPD in December 1964. Behind is another of the same class, with a 2–6–4T standing beyond. Piles of ash and clinker lie beside the track. These would be shovelled into a wagon in due course and removed, the material often being used for filling slips in embankments.

Laurence Waters Collection/D. Tuck

An atmospheric scene inside the shed at Dumfries, showing the last remaining Caledonian Railway 19 class 0–4–4T No. 55124 at the front. One of the first designs of J.F. McIntosh, in 1895, this type had smaller side tanks and coal rails around the top of the bunker. No. 55124 managed to retain its original pattern of chimney, the engine being sixty years old when this photograph was taken on 8.9.58.

David Fereday Glenn

Crewe had two locomotive sheds: Crewe North dealing largely with passenger engines, and Crewe South housing freight locomotives to deal with traffic emanating from the huge marshalling yards there. In addition, there was the locomotive construction works, established by the London and North Western Railway in the 1840s and responsible for building many famous engines, including, in 1934, 4–6–0 No. 45552 *Silver Jubilee*, seen here outside Crewe North shed in 1964.

Mike Hitches Collection/Terry Roberts

Great Northern Railway (Ireland) SG3 class 0–6–0 No. 47 stands in heavy rain outside Adelaide shed, Belfast with sister locomotive No. 48 alongside. Within the shed were twenty-eight more steam engines, and a diesel railcar and twin-car outside at the rear. No. 47 was withdrawn in 1965 and No. 48 in 1968. This view was taken on 22.4.65.

Maurice Dart

Ex-NCC WT class 2–6–4T No. 10 at York Road, Belfast on 23.3.70. This engine is a modified version of similar locomotives Fowler built for the LMS, though adapted to the Irish track gauge. Some features of the Fowler design have been modified: the top of the bunker has been inset to give a better view to the rear, and a gap left between the buffer beam and running plate to give extra access to the steam chest. These machines had distinct NCC features, such as cast number plates on their bunkers, and smokebox door wheels.

These Irish engines were familiarly known as 'Jeeps'. In 1965 No. 55 was experimentally fitted with a tender to augment its water supply and in this condition worked one or two trips to Dublin. The last duties of this class were hauling motorway spoil trains, usually powered by an engine at each end.

Colin G. Maggs

W class 2–6–0 No. 97 *Earl of Ulster*, built at Derby by the LMS for its Northern Counties Committee line which had the Irish standard gauge of 5 ft 3 in. *Earl of Ulster* had been withdrawn from service and stood outside York Road locomotive works, Belfast, in a torrential downpour on 22.4.65. To the right, a boiler stands on a works wagon. Five other members of the class were seen by the photographer that afternoon, withdrawn and stored inside Adelaide shed, Belfast.

Maurice Dart

Locomotives in the Town

A pair of class 5 4–6–0s, Nos. 45247 and 45005, prepare to leave Penmaenmawr granite sidings with ballast trains during the late 1950s. With the demise of steam traction, these duties were taken over by class 24 and class 25 Bo-Bo or class 40 Co-Co diesel-electrics. Railway ballast is still produced at Penmaenmawr and several trains still call at the sidings every day for loading, usually hauled by class 31 or class 47 diesel-electrics.

Mike Hitches Collection/Gwyn Roberts

THE RAILWAY SCENE IN MANY TOWNS has been transformed over the last thirty years. Today goods yards have almost disappeared, but in the past were very busy places, with wagons being shunted before and after emptying, and goods being transferred between platform and wagon or vice versa, in the open air or under cover depending on the durability of the item. Today most of the freight carried by rail is in bulk, the whole train proceeding to one destination. Thirty years ago most towns had at least one engine at work in the yard for most, if not all, of the day and night. As well as goods arriving by freight train, some for speedy delivery arrived as tail traffic on passenger trains, and these vehicles needed shunting on and off.

Cattle pens were a common feature, and often the cattle trucks needed cleaning and disinfecting. Coal and coke provided important traffic in the days when most people had at least one open fire in their home. Then there were the specialized items dealt with by the town: raw materials for factories and the end products being despatched. A large factory usually had its own private siding. Often customers were required to clear wagons of their consignments. A 'free period' of forty-eight hours was allowed for a wagon to be emptied, increased to seventy-two hours for coal and coke. If a wagon had not been emptied in this time, a daily demurrage charge was incurred – a quite fair imposition as a wagon still under load deprived the railway of its use and therefore led to loss of revenue.

Some towns had a large marshalling yard where wagons from various stations in the district were shunted to form trains going to various destinations. Sometimes they were flat yards, while at others an engine pushed wagons over a hump, from which they ran down the other side by gravity into sidings, each for a different destination. A marshalling yard had two main parts: the reception roads into which trains were run on arrival, and the sorting sidings into which the wagons were eventually run. With this layout of reception road, hump and sorting sidings, long trains could be shunted much more quickly than with ordinary flat shunting, where an engine had to be continually stopping and reversing as wagons were shunted off the end of the rake. A flat yard took an hour to shunt about seventy wagons; a hump yard could perform this operation in about 7 minutes.

Hump yards were often equipped with retarders in order to keep an appropriate distance between successive wagons and to let them enter a siding at a suitable speed to reach other wagons already there, but not buffer up too harshly. Where a hump yard was not fitted with retarders, wagon brakes had to be applied by hand, which required a large staff and a certain risk to life and limb. Shunting wagons was rather hard on the vehicles. Sometimes they crashed rather heavily into each other, causing damage additional to normal wear and tear, so large stations usually had a wagon repair depot.

Some yards had sidings accessed via short turntables, and horses were used for shunting wagons on sidings of this type, though latterly BSA Cycles Ltd developed a truck mover self-propelled by an air-cooled engine which also operated a powerful hydraulic ram that locked the truck mover securely between the rail and a wagon's underframe. The truck mover was fitted with solid rubber tyres on its two steel wheels.

Enginemen had to take precautions in towns which were unnecessary in the country. For example, it was frowned upon to let an engine blow off in a station, particularly if it was in a train shed, because apart from the waste of coal and water it made a loud noise, making speech and listening to the public-address system impossible. If in the vicinity of a hospital, drivers had to keep their engine as quiet as possible. Priming in towns could cause problems. One fireman preparing an engine turned an injector on and then went off to get another engine ready, completely forgetting to check the state of the water level in the boiler of the first. His driver, while going round oiling, also failed to notice that the injector had been on for a lengthy period, so that when the time came for them to leave the shed, the engine travelled on hydraulic power rather than steam. Black, sooty water poured from the chimney and seemed to go everywhere. On this beautiful summer day they crossed an overbridge, under which a lady was walking in a light-coloured frock . . . the result can be imagined!

In the days of steam there was a considerable amount of engine-changing at many town stations, particularly if they happened to be termini, or at the junctions between two British Railway regions. Today there is far less, due to diesel or electric locomotives being capable of running much longer distances without servicing, and the use of double-ended units obviating the need for a locomotive to run round its train at a terminus.

As well as being a seaside resort, Penmaenmawr was famed for the granite quarried from the mountain visible in this view. From 1888 the London and North Western Railway began to use stone hewn from Penmaenmawr Mountain for railway ballast, with initial orders for nearly three million tons. To supply the railway, the quarry company constructed an extensive sidings complex behind the railway station to load railway wagons. These were still being very well used in this early-1960s view of BR Standard class 9F 2–10–0 No. 92203 of 8A (Edge Hill) awaiting departure at the head of a train of loaded ballast wagons. In the background can be seen loading hoppers used to store the stone until required. The locomotive has been preserved by wildlife painter David Shepherd, who has named it *Black Prince*. It operates on the East Somerset Railway.

Mike Hitches Collection / Gwyn Roberts

Class 2P 4–4–0 No. 40537 and BR Standard class 5 No. 73019 with the 'Pines Express', tackling the start of the 1 in 50 gradient over the Mendips on 28.3.59. Most passenger trains of any length required assistance between Bath and Evercreech Junction. The first engine belonged to the LMS, whereas the site of the photograph, Bath Junction, was neither London, Midland nor Scottish! On the left is Bath gasworks which received forty wagons of coal daily, or 3200 tons per week, all by rail. The fireman of No. 73019 is retrieving the single line tablet from the catcher on the tender.

Colin G. Maggs

Class 5 4–6–0 No. 44997 leaving Grangemouth docks with a fitted freight train in August 1959.

R.E. Toop

Class 4F 0–6–0 No. 44135 approaches the Somerset and Dorset single line at Bath Junction on 28.3.59, working the 3.20 p.m. Bath Green Park to Templecombe. As this engine was not fitted with a tablet-catcher, the fireman dangerously hangs out to snatch the pouch from the lineside apparatus. Had the signalman been informed that this locomotive was not fitted with a catcher, he would have placed the tablet in a pouch with a larger handle.

Signalmen at Bath Junction box were susceptible to colds through having to make frequent journeys into the fresh air to either set up or collect a tablet. Bath Junction was also unique among S&D single-line boxes in having to deal with banking engine staff.

No. 44135 is hauling SR coach set 447. This was in its last weeks of service as it had been withdrawn by July 1959.

Colin G. Maggs

Reading gasworks on Sunday 3.3.63, with BR Standard class 5 4–6–0 No. 73085 *Melisande* shunting the Nine Elms breakdown train prior to the unloading of a gas condenser. The latter had arrived by road from Aldershot before being taken to Reading South station for loading on to a railway wagon for the short journey to the gasworks. *Melisande* received its name from a withdrawn 'King Arthur' class engine.

Kevin Robertson Collection/G.R. May

Stamford was blessed with two railway stations, just a stone's throw from each other. Midland trains ran east and west, while the Great Northern ran north and south. This urban scene is on the approach to the GNR station, an interesting terminus known as Stamford Town in its latter days. The locomotive in charge of the lonesome brake van is class 8F 2–8–0 No. 48752 and the date is 20.3.63. The engine was built by the LNER during the Second World War to Stanier's design. The sooted wooden signal gantry with its brackets, the arched masonry of bridge 66, and the swan-necked water crane all provide a strong pictorial framework for the train, but the real showpiece is the neat suspended signal.

Alan Postlethwaite

Several impressive signal gantries can be seen in this photograph taken at Tyne dock on 7.7.56; note too, the elevated signal-box.

The locomotive at the head of one of the Consett iron ore block trains is O1 class 2–8–0 No. 63856. Engines used on these duties were fitted with Westinghouse air pumps in front of the cab. This equipment operated the 56 ton hopper wagons. Other locomotives used on this duty included Q7 class 0–8–0s and BR Standard class 9F 2–10–0s which were similarly fitted.

Many O4 class locomotives were rebuilt by Thompson as O1s, the first appearing in 1944. Among the major changes were fitting 100A-type boilers, new cylinders and Walschaerts valve gear. The O1s were among the last heavy freight steam locomotives used further south on the Eastern Region, prior to complete dieselization.

E.H. Sawford

Seldom photographed, William Worsdell's 4–8–0T design for the North Eastern Railway had three cylinders and was introduced in 1909 for heavy shunting and freight work. By the 1950s the T1 class was in terminal decline, many of its duties being taken over by new BR standard diesel shunting engines. The last survivors of the T1 class were found at Tyne dock, where on 2.9.58 No. 69920 drifted past gantries of old NER signals close to the locomotive depot coded 52H. Note the lack of vacuum brake pipes and a simple three-link coupling, as befitted a purely freight engine.

David Fereday Glenn

For a great many years the heavy Continental boat trains were worked over the Folkestone Harbour branch by veteran R1 class 0–6–0Ts. Folkestone Junction shed had seven of these locomotives, principally for these duties. All were officially allocated to Dover, as Folkestone was a sub-shed, without its own allocation. Working a heavy boat train up the gradient of 1 in 30 to Folkestone Junction was difficult. Usually there were three locomotives at the head of the train, with a fourth banking at the rear.

Here Nos 31337, 31047 and 31069 start out from the Harbour station and cross the swing bridge, with No. 31107 assisting at the rear. Although steam engines were the usual motive power in those days, the sight and sounds of a boat train leaving with four engines always attracted the attention of passers-by.

E.H. Sawford

Locomotives in the Country

H class 0–4–4T No. 31177 at Dunton Green on 4.4.59 with the 11.50 a.m. to Westerham. It hauled the train one way and pushed it in the reverse direction to obviate the time and trouble of running round at the end of each journey. The pipes for the air operation of the controls used by the driver when in the control vestibule of the coach can be seen to the right of the coupling hook. The track on the right is electrified. No. 31177 was allocated to 74D (Tonbridge).

Colin G. Maggs

The church spire at Oundle points in the opposite direction to the lower quadrant railway signal apparently suspended in space. On this overcast day, the exhaust steam from class B1 4–6–0 No. 61059 blends imperceptibly with the grey sky. The train is on the down gradient of 1 in 212 from Oundle station, on the London and North Western Railway's line from Northampton to Peterborough, on 22.3.63. It is clearly a 'fair trot' from the station to the town centre.

Alan Postlethwaite

OBSERVING TRAINS IN THE COUNTRY was a pastime of great contrasts. There would be birdsong, the hum of insects, the drone of a tractor, or maybe a plane. Then a plume of steam would appear. Was it a passenger or goods train? What was the engine? Would it be a 'foreign' engine hauling the train? Would it be a rare engine from a distant shed? Would there be something particularly interesting on the train – a bullion van, Royal Mail van with pick-up apparatus, or maybe an industrial engine being worked 'dead'? The train would pass, quickly or slowly, four-wheeled wagons tapping out an exciting rhythm if going quickly and bogie wagons causing an exciting interval. The questions posed would be answered and the countryside settled down again to its natural sounds.

If the observer was near a signal-box, there would be an additional stage in the pattern of excitement. A block bell would ring and if the enthusiast was knowledgeable enough, he would be able to determine whether it was an Up or Down train and what type it was. A less skilful observer would have to wait and see which signals were

pulled off and curb his impatience until the train could be identified by sight.

Grassed-over cuttings and embankments became an integral part of the countryside, with a wealth of wild flowers, insects and small animals – in fact, linear nature reserves. One duty of the permanent way staff in steam days was to cut this growth alongside the track to prevent it catching alight from a spark, and in turn setting trees, hay or a cornfield on fire. This grass was sometimes sold to smallholders in return for beer money, or burned in a controlled manner. On one occasion when carrying out this last procedure, a cherry tree in a neighbouring garden went up in flames, the owner successfully claiming £14 damages from British Railways. A few years later the tree's owner saw the men and asked if they would burn it down again, as this caused it to give a heavier crop.

Being a country signalman away from a station could be rather lonely, but there was nature to observe, and passing permanent way men to chat to. One signalman, keen on fishing and whose box was close to a stream,

manufactured a 20 ft-long rod in order to enjoy piscatorial pursuits while at work. The same ingenious signalman worked in a box which had electricity – quite unusual in country boxes – so he purchased an electric radio, drilled a hole through the floor to an electric socket in the locking room below and plugged his wireless in. He used a crocodile clip to attach the aerial to a telephone wire and got marvellous reception. Unfortunately, the radio signals travelled along the wire to District Control, which put a stop to his entertainment!

Signal-boxes were usually heated by coal, but the quantity issued was not always sufficient, so various ploys were used in order to augment supplies. One signalman's trick was to unhitch a signal wire when a light engine was belled, thus rendering the signal inoperable. The light engine had to stop and be given a written order allowing it to pass the signal at danger. The driver was invited to come into the box while the order was being written out, and when there was asked if he would tell his fireman to throw some coal from the tender. About

10 cwt was thrown out, the engine proceeded and the wire was reconnected.

If a railway ran through or beside a gentleman's estate, there was the opportunity to enjoy game, legally or otherwise. Occasionally a pheasant would be struck by the smokebox door and could be retrieved from the buffer beam, while at other times the footplate crew might be tempted to poach. This happened at Stanton Great Wood, a pheasant covert beside the Swindon to Highworth line, where a lump of coal was aimed at a bird from a passing locomotive. The men were unable to pick up their prey on that journey but stopped on the next. Just as the fireman was about to pick up his prize, it was jerked away by the gamekeeper who had watched the whole episode. When questioned by the railway authorities, the footplatemen denied that coal had been misappropriated, but this was hard to believe when no fewer than five sackfuls were recovered from the lineside!

Gradients, whether up or down, caused problems for drivers of goods trains without continuous brakes, the only brakes being on the engine, tender and brake van.

During the summer months the North Wales Coast line received excursion trains from the north of England, the Midlands and even from as far distant as Scotland. On 27.7.63 Eastern Region's Thompson B1 class 4–6–0 No. 61249 *FitzHerbert Wright* heads an excursion train from the North-East through Deganwy on is way to Llandudno. This class was by no means a rarity on the North Wales Coast line.

Mike Hitches Collection/Peter Owen

The GWR had 'Stop & Pin Down Brakes' boards at the head of its steep gradients, but the LMS and Somerset and Dorset usually managed to operate their trains down gradients without this time-consuming precaution, and runaways, although not unknown, were infrequent. This method of operation led to spectacular night-time scenes, with the tyres of a brake van and locomotive glowing red-hot, crews saying that at night they gave so much light that 'You could see rabbits playing in the fields.' One driver observed, 'It's like Brock's Benefit Night with fire and flames coming off the locomotive and tender wheels, and all the guard's wheels and blocks red-hot. Sheets of flame; great Catherine wheels.'

Climbing a gradient could be tricky. If a banking engine was unavailable, arrangements were made with Control or a signalman to make sure a clear road was available and the heavy train would not be held on a bank by adverse signals, faced with the impossible task of restarting. One such incident occurred during the Second World War, Driver Bob Ford recording:

A Down train arrived at Gloucester headed by an 8F, almost brand-new. The driver and fireman said, 'You've got a special lot here.' The train consisted of forty American box cars, big things, six-wheelers. I suppose they must have weighed fifteen to twenty tons each and their contents I was not allowed to reveal, but I was ordered: 'Under no circumstances emit sparks.' I knew what I was carrying, but that wasn't for publication.

Immediately we'd finished taking on water I said to Bernard West, my fireman, 'Have a look in the box, drive the dart through and build yourself a good fire and I'll have a word with Control.' I went over and told them, 'You know about this sealed-orders train I've got here with American box cars. Well, I'm only a young driver and although I know the road like the back of my hand, I'm not going to lift these out of here up a gradient of 1 in 108 without a banker, so where is it?' 'Oh, it's in Gloucester shed having its fire cleaned and I think the set of men who were on it have gone home,' came the reply. 'Well,' I insisted, 'get another set of men on. Get the banker out. I've a forty-load here and I reckon it weighs anything up to 1500 tons. That's only an estimate, I don't know what's in these box vans.' 'Oh,' came the reply, so I continued, 'I've 1500 tons and I'm against the collar to Tuffley as you know very well.' 'We'll see what we can do, driver.'

Ten minutes went by and as no assistance appeared I went back to Control and asked, 'What on earth's happening over this lot?' They answered, 'We can't get you a banker, there are no men available.' I responded sharply. 'Are you telling me I've got to take this forty-load on my own up the bank?' 'Well, we don't know,' came the hesitant reply. 'Well I do,' I replied, 'and I'll tell you what. I'll take them seeing that it's an 8 Freight and she should be pretty powerful. I'll take them if you'll guarantee the road to Tuffley, so if I'm checked, you'll have the responsibility of getting the banker out and shoving me from a standstill.' After a few moments' consultation came the reply, 'We'll do that.' I said, 'That's fair enough then, I'll risk my neck and take them.'

Control kept its word and Driver Ford's skill enabled him to climb the gradient.

The versatile J15 class 0–6–0s were introduced by Worsdell for the Great Eastern Railway in 1883, yet many were still to be found at a number of Eastern Region depots in East Anglia and the London area during the fifties. One depot which had an allocation of ten in 1954 was Cambridge. The duties worked by this class involved both passenger and goods traffic. Cambridge J15s worked passenger trains over the Mildenhall branch, the Colne Valley line and, perhaps most surprisingly, an early morning passenger train to Kettering, returning home with the last train of the day. For many years the regular engine for this train was No. 65390, although others did appear on occasion.

Another duty was the 'Huntingdon Pilot', a J15 being outstationed at the small sub-shed there for a ten-day period. This locomotive worked goods traffic between Huntingdon and St Ives, and also carried out shunting work at both locations, even for a short period working a goods train on the East Coast main line as far as St Neots. On at least one occasion when on this duty, the J15 was commandeered to take over an express, struggling as far as St Neots before a larger engine relieved it for the rest of the journey to King's Cross.

In this photograph No. 65442 stands in Huntingdon yard on 25.8.54.

E.H. Sawford

The Gresley A4 Pacifics were responsible for working most of the principal express trains on the East Coast main line until superseded by diesel-electrics, mainly class 40s and 'Deltics', which themselves are now history. Many of the A4s worked trains between Aberdeen and Glasgow in their last years of service. King's Cross depot, frequently referred to as 'Top Shed', had the largest allocation. In 1954 nineteen locomotives were based there, with the remaining fifteen at Edinburgh and Newcastle-upon-Tyne. Those at London included such famous names as *Sir Nigel Gresley, Silver Link* and the legendary *Mallard*. No. 60026 *Miles Beevor* was also a King's Cross engine and is seen here, south of Huntingdon, at the head of an express bound for the capital. Six examples of the thirty-four-strong class survive.

E.H. Sawford

Until the sixties there remained across Kent, Sussex and Surrey a network of interconnecting branch and secondary routes which were still largely the preserve of steam. One such, with an hourly-interval service for much of the day, was between Three Bridges and East Grinstead, a 6¾ mile-long single line with passing places at Rowfant and Grange Road. Regular as clockwork, a two-coach push-pull train handled this operation, here exemplified by class H 0–4–4T No. 31278 heading for Three Bridges with the 3.27 p.m. from East Grinstead on 14.3.62. Built in 1905 for the South Eastern and Chatham Railway, No. 31278 glints in the sunshine as it bustles away from Rowfant station amid the serried ranks of silver birch trees.

David Fereday Glenn

Passenger services between Petersfield, Midhurst and Pulborough were axed in February 1955, but freight traffic continued to serve Midhurst, Selham, Petworth and Fittleworth from Pulborough for some years. Motive power for this service, which ran once each way on weekdays only, was provided by Horsham or Three Bridges sheds. As the locomotive was almost invariably of pre-Grouping origin, the character of the operation hardly changed through the years. On 16.6.61 class C2X 0–6–0 No. 32534 emerges into the sylvan surroundings of Cowdray Park with the 12.30 p.m. pick-up goods from Midhurst to Pulborough, leaving the claustrophobic confines of Midhurst tunnel behind. The last class C2X went to the scrapyard in early 1962, and Midhurst finally succumbed to closure in the autumn of 1964.

David Fereday Glenn

BR Standard class 4 2–6–0 No. 76065 at Cole, Somerset, on 28.10.61, heading the 1.10 p.m. Bournemouth West to Bath Green Park. It is seen here crossing the ex-GWR line to the west of England. The train consists of ex-GWR coaches.

There is an interesting variety of fence posts. To the left is one made from old bridge rail, while those in the centre are made from wood. The latter tended to ignite when sparks from a passing locomotive set light to the neighbouring grass, so for this reason they were replaced by more durable concrete posts, which can be seen on the other side of the track.

Colin G. Maggs

An almost-forgotten relic of the GWR's territorial ambitions of a bygone age lingered into the sixties with the use of a Western Region engine to work one train in each direction on weekdays between Reading and Redhill. On 10.1.62 43XX class 2–6–0 No. 6379 of 81D (Reading) blasts away from Gomshall and Shere station with the 12.35 p.m. from Redhill, bound for Guildford, North Camp, Wokingham and Reading, with Southern green coaches behind the tender. Note the WR headlamps on the position that would signify an express passenger train on the locomotive's home territory, but which on the SR indicated the route.

David Fereday Glenn

Passengers travelling by the 3.15 p.m. from Paddington could enjoy the comfort of a restaurant car before alighting from the Oxford train at Reading, where a stopping service to Trowbridge departed at 4.07 p.m. 'Modified Hall' class 4–6–0 No. 7921 *Edstone Hall* of 81A (Old Oak Common) was in charge on 31.3.62 as the Trowbridge train emerged from the ornate tunnel into Devizes station a little behind schedule. The line closed completely from 18.4.66.

David Fereday Glenn

The 12½ mile-long branch from Newton Abbot to Moretonhampstead lost its passenger service from the beginning of March 1959, but freight traffic continued throughout for a few years before being cut back, first to Bovey and then to Heathfield. On Easter Eve, 16.4.60, a pick-up goods ran to Moretonhampstead and spent some time shunting. For the return journey to Newton Abbot the load consisted of a single wooden-bodied coal wagon and the usual brake van. Class 45XX 2–6–2T No. 4555 ambled along in leisurely fashion past milepost 11¼ on the fringe of Dartmoor between Moretonhampstead and Lustleigh with its lightweight train. Saved by the Dart Valley Railway in the mid-1960s, this locomotive has returned to Devon and is the oldest survivor of its type.

David Fereday Glenn

'Modified Hall' class 4–6–0 No. 7909 *Heveningham Hall*, of 83A (Newton Abbot), passes over Sodbury troughs on the Wootton Bassett to Filton line, Avon, with a Down goods on 15.6.62. At this point there was water below the engine and water above, for the black bridge on slender brick piers supported an aqueduct. Beyond the second overbridge is the portal of Chipping Sodbury tunnel, 2 miles 926 yd in length beneath the Cotswolds; a castellated ventilation shaft can be seen just below the summit of the hill. To the right of the buffer beam is a bin holding small ballast for packing under sleepers. No. 7909 was withdrawn in November 1965.

Colin G. Maggs

The view from the fireman's window of 14XX class 0–4–2T No. 1472 as it approached Ham Mill halt with a Gloucester to Chalford stopping train on 18.4.63. One platform of the halt can be seen immediately to the right of the chimney. The low boiler gives the crew almost as good visibility as on a diesel. The line curves its way up through the Golden Valley before penetrating the Cotswold Hills via Sapperton tunnel. On the right is a permanent way hut. No. 1472 was withdrawn in November 1964.

Colin G. Maggs

Class 28XX 2–8–0 No. 3820 of 81E (Didcot) at Standish on the Gloucester to Swindon line. Note the bars strengthening the buffer beam. Steam issues from the safety valve surrounded by a cover, as was GWR practice. The coupling is neatly slung on its hook. Some of the vans are ventilated, the sloping rectangle admitting air to the interior. Parallel with the ex-GWR line at this point is the ex-LMS Gloucester to Bristol line. The quadruple track was reduced to double in 1968. No. 3820 was withdrawn in October 1965.

Colin G. Maggs

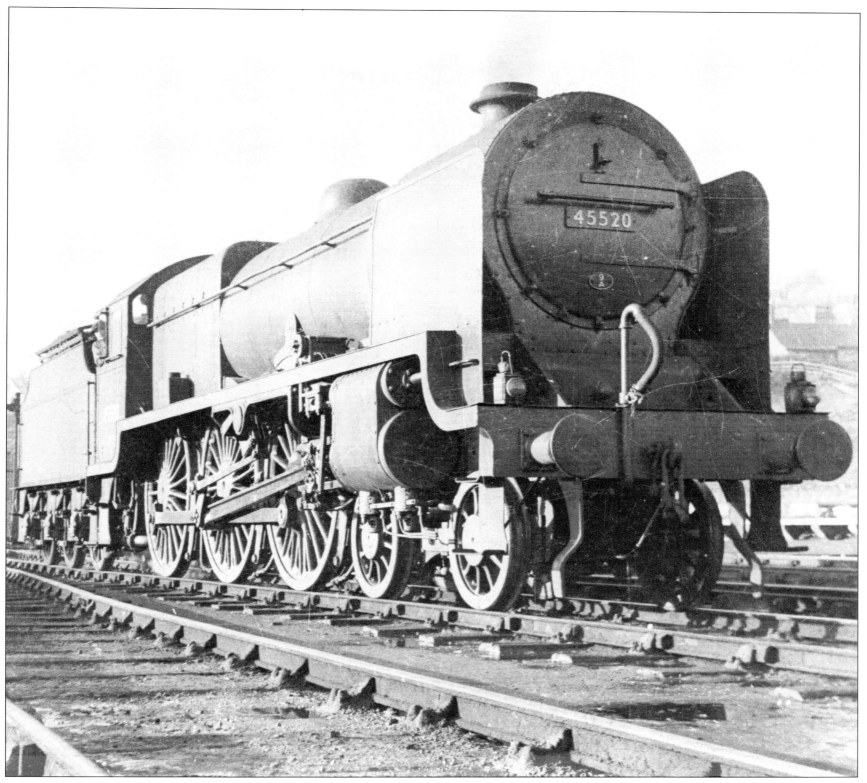

Resting on the shed road at Bangor in the early 1960s is unrebuilt 'Patriot' class 4–6–0 No. 45520 *Llandudno*. Bangor was an important terminus for many local services, as well as dealing with express traffic to and from Holyhead, Euston, Birmingham, Manchester and Liverpool. Trains ran along the branch to Afonwen, where the LMS joined the GWR's Cambrian Coast line from Shrewsbury to Pwllheli. Many excursions from Manchester and Liverpool to Butlin's holiday camp at Penychain, near Pwllheli, used this route, calling at Bangor to change the locomotive. Bangor's role was gradually reduced from 1951, when the branch to the slate quarrying town of Bethesda was closed, but the station was even more greatly affected by the closure of the Amlwch branch on Anglesey, and the line between Caernarfon and Afonwen in 1964 following publication of the Beeching Report. The section between Bangor and Caernarfon closed in 1970, leaving Bangor to deal only with main-line traffic. With these closures, Bangor also lost its locomotive shed, there no longer being a demand for engines.

Mike Hitches Collection / Gwyn Roberts

The 'straight and simple' track layout at Llanfyllin was designed for goods traffic somewhat heavier than suggested by this single-van pick-up freight train. In the heart of central Wales, this branch terminus was attractively set on the edge of a village whose homes and church tower are just visible in the background. The wooden advance starter signal is of Cambrian Railways pattern, but the home signals are pure GWR. The locomotive is ex-LMS class 2 2–6–0 No. 46519 and the date is 9.6.62.

Alan Postlethwaite

Class 8F 2–8–0 No. 48737 of 82F (Bath Green Park) heads into the evening sunlight on the edge of Kelston Park, west of Bath, with a freight to Birmingham on 6.6.64. Smoke from the chimney indicates that the fire is being prepared for the 4 mile-long bank through Bitton and Warmley with a ruling gradient of 1 in 121.

Colin G. Maggs

One of the ubiquitous 'Black Five' 4–6–0s, No. 45275, heads a Down express beside the shore towards Penmaenmawr on a summer day in 1964, about a year before steam disappeared from the north Wales coast.

Quite apart from the loss of steam traction in the area, there have been other changes. The grassy area on the left has all been eroded away by the action of the sea, and the road on the right has been considerably widened in recent years as part of the development of the A55 expressway to relieve chronic traffic jams that have become a major problem since the days of steam.

Mike Hitches Collection/Peter Owen

BR Standard Pacific of the 'Britannia' class, No. 70031 *Byron*, bursts out of Penmaenbach tunnel, about 5 miles west of Llandudno Junction, with a Holyhead to Manchester express on 21.7.62. This locomotive, then un-named, first appeared on the North Wales Coast line in 1954, being one of the first five assigned to haul the 'Irish Mail', but was quickly withdrawn when it was found that its BR1-type tender, still fitted in this view, proved not to have the capacity to cope with the demands of the long run. *Byron*, together with the other four of the class allocated to the 'Irish Mail', was transferred to Longsight, Manchester, from where it then operated. These five 'Britannias' were replaced by Nos 70045–49, which were fitted with the larger BR1D tenders more suited to the demands of the Holyhead to Euston service.

Mike Hitches Collection / Peter Owen

Hard at work on a 1 in 60 gradient, a post-Grouping development of the Caledonian Railway's 439 class, 0–4–4T No. 55236, climbs slowly towards Killin Junction with the 1.42 p.m. from Killin on 5.9.60. Its chimney is of the stovepipe pattern. The ballast is unusually weedy.

David Fereday Glenn

'Jubilee' class 4–6–0 No. 45717 *Dauntless* of 27A (Bank Hall) nears Beattock summit up a gradient of 1 in 99 with the 11.10 a.m. Edinburgh to Liverpool on 17.8.61. A pile of small stone ballast for packing under sleepers can be seen on the left. This line has been electrified now for many years.

Colin G. Maggs

Narrow Gauge Locomotives and Industrials

A veteran saddle tank with only a rudimentary cab affording little protection from the elements for the driver, hauls a van train across High Street in the centre of Burton-on-Trent, bringing traffic to a halt. The locomotive, Worthington No. 6, was in an immaculate blue livery, adorned with red lining and a glistening brass dome. This 0–4–0ST was built by Hudswell Clarke in 1920, works No. 1417, and sold for scrap in 1960. The picture was taken on 17.9.58.

Maurice Dart

NARROW-GAUGE LINES HAVE THE ADVANTAGE of being able to negotiate smaller radius curves than a standard-gauge line and so are particularly useful in hilly or mountainous country where they can follow the contours, thus avoiding expensive cuttings and embankments. Additional advantages are that they require rather less land and the rolling stock is smaller and cheaper, so less unladen weight needs to be carried if traffic is light. Wagons can be moved easily by hand if necessary – not an easy procedure with a standard-gauge wagon. At one time there were quite a few narrow-gauge railways in mid- and north Wales, of which several, but not all, used the 1 ft 11½ in gauge. The Welshpool and Llanfair Railway, built to the 2 ft 6 in gauge, opened in 1903 and was worked by the Cambrian Railways, absorbed by the GWR in 1922. The latter company 'Great Westernized' the two 0–6–0Ts *The Earl* and *The Countess*. Passenger services over the line were withdrawn in 1931 due to bus competition, but goods working continued until 1956, it being the second and last narrow-gauge line to be closed by British Railways. Fortunately, it was taken over by a preservation society.

The first railway in the Isle of Man ran from Douglas to Peel and was opened in 1873 on a 3 ft gauge, which was adopted for the island. The original 2–4–0T engines remained standard until 1926, when a similar, though larger, engine of the same wheel arrangement was placed in service. Lines were subsequently opened to Port Erin, Ramsey and Foxdale. A 3 ft gauge electric railway, its design owing much to street tramways rather than railways, ran from Douglas to Groundle Glen in 1893 and was extended to Ramsey in 1899. The associated 3 ft 6 in gauge Snaefell Mountain Railway opened in 1894. Until the 1960s, railways on the island flourished, as they suffered little competition, having absorbed the rival road transport companies in 1929. Until recently, few of the thousands of tourists visiting the island brought their own cars, so the railway, with low fares and an excellent service, reaped a good harvest.

In their heyday, Britain's industrial railways received little attention from enthusiasts because they were not considered as glamorous as top-flight expresses; bigger and newer was thought to be better, and smaller and older, worse. Fortunately, a few far-sighted people took an interest in these Cinderella railways, some of which were largely inaccessible to the public. Until the sixties, most collieries, gas- and electricity-generating stations, ironworks, quarries and heavy industries owned an industrial line, often linking with British Railways, but sometimes independent and occasionally narrow gauge.

Industrial railways tended to use tank engines, usually of the saddle tank variety with 0–4–0 or 0–6–0 wheel arrangements, tender engines being very rare. Some industrial railways were worked by a Fordson tractor, the rails having to be inset and their top surface level with the ground. The introduction of North Sea gas put paid to gasworks lines, as there was no need to bring in numerous coal trucks. Beckton gasworks in London had thirty-four locomotives, over a thousand wagons and 70 miles of track. The Manchester Ship Canal had 212 route miles of rail, over two thousand wagons and seventy-four steam locomotives. However, industrial lines did not just use old designs: the first Beyer-Garratt articulated locomotive to work in Great Britain was an 0–4–0+0–4–0T purchased by Messrs Vivian and Sons of Swansea in 1923.

A type confined to industrial railways was the fireless steam locomotive. In chemical works, oil refineries and places where sparks would be dangerous, fireless engines were used. In appearance they were like a conventional locomotive without a chimney. What appeared to be a boiler and firebox was really just a steam container, though still surmounted by a dome and safety valve. This steam container could supply steam to the cylinders for several hours. It was filled with high-temperature water to about three-quarters of its capacity and the remaining space was charged with superheated steam from a stationary boiler. Matters were arranged so that steam, on entering the container, was mixed with the hot water, the effect of which increased the pressure, thus remedying a certain loss occurring in the charging process.

Sometimes industrial railways used a self-propelled steam crane for shunting, while others used crane engines which were conventional steam engines fitted with a small crane. Another type of unconventional steam locomotive was the Sentinel geared locomotive with a vertical boiler. This boiler was sited in the cab, while the space normally occupied by a conventional boiler was taken up with the locomotive's cylinders. These engines were fast-revving, and both looked and sounded like diesels.

Most of the last steam-worked industrial lines in Britain belonged to the NCB, which naturally liked using its own fuel to provide motive power, but a few other concerns hung on to their steamers for a few years after British Railways withdrew theirs, simply because the steam engine was a relatively simple machine to maintain and proved most reliable.

Of 2 ft 6 in gauge, 0–6–0T No. 822, previously named *The Earl*, was built by Beyer Peacock in 1902 for the Welshpool and Llanfair Railway. This company was absorbed by the GWR, eventually becoming one of British Railways' narrow-gauge lines. Here, No. 822 stands at Welshpool on 15.9.56, opposite the main-line station and heading the penultimate BR train over the line, run on behalf of the Branch Line Society. The Welshpool and Llanfair Railway has been preserved and this locomotive is still in running order.

Maurice Dart

Gwent, an 0–6–0ST, at Hafodyrynys colliery, Pontypool in February 1968. Its name is painted on the saddle tank. This locomotive was built by Hunslet in 1952, works No. 3780. One engine was usually in steam, with the other, on this occasion *Glendower* (Hunslet Works No. 3810 of 1954), spare. Notice its striped buffer beam to give greater visual warning of its approach. On the left is a GWR 4-mile post.

Colin G. Maggs Collection / W.H. Harbor

An exciting scene near St John's station on the Isle of Man on 2.9.60. The three-coach train on the left, headed by 2–4–0T No. 8 *Fenella*, is for Ramsey, while No. 14 *Thornhill*, with the same wheel arrangement, descends to Peel. Unofficial racing over this parallel stretch was not entirely unknown. Note that No. 8 has its number fixed to the side of the chimney.

Alan Postlethwaite

A subtropical setting for an immaculate train at Sulby Bridge station on the Manx Northern line to Ramsey on 2.9.60. The glistening dome belongs to 2–4–0T No. 13 *Kissack*.

Alan Postlethwaite

A busy scene on 31.8.60 outside the engine shed at Douglas, Isle of Man, with 2–4–0T No. 16 *Mannin* on the left, and 2–4–0Ts Nos 6 *Peveril*, 10 *G.H. Wood*, 11 *Maitland* and 13 *Kissack*. Note that the tank filler is inside the cab. The gauge is 3 ft. At one time having a route mileage of 46, only the 15½ miles from Douglas to Port Erin have been preserved.

Alan Postlethwaite

A few British Railways steam locomotives enjoyed a new lease of life working elsewhere. Here 57XX class 0–6–0PT No. 9600 is seen at Merthyr Vale colliery in July 1970. Sold to the National Coal Board in September 1965, it remained in use at Merthyr Vale until April 1973. This colliery had two engines in steam and one spare.

Colin G. Maggs Collection/W.H. Harbor

An NCB 0–6–0ST shunting at Maesteg colliery in August 1970. Some industrial locations were quite photogenic. The colliery had six steam engines, of which half were usually working at any one time.

Colin G. Maggs Collection/W.H. Harbor

Last Trains and Locomotive Scrapping

S15 class 4–6–0 No. 30499 waits at Feltham shed in June 1964 for the call to the scrapyard. Two other members of the class were marshalled ready for departure – Nos 30841 and 30847. The removal of coupling and connecting rods was a sure sign of condemnation. Fortunately, No. 30499 survived to be preserved on the Watercress Line.

Kevin Robertson Collection/J.R. Fairman

133

End of the line at Swindon on 28.4.63. 'King' class 4–6–0 No. 6018 *King Henry VI*, on the left, and No. 6026 *King John*, on the right, on the occasion of the final run of No. 6018 at the head of a Stephenson Locomotive Society special working. Originally numbering thirty, most of the class was withdrawn in 1962, but No. 6018 was specially reinstated for this SLS working. Sadly, this was to prove its final steaming and both engines were destined for the cutter's torch.

Kevin Robertson Collection/J.R. Fairman

MID-DECEMBER 1947 SAW THE APPEARANCE of Britain's first main-line diesel-electric locomotive, LMS No. 10000. This was followed in 1951 by Southern Region No. 10201. A gas-turbine locomotive ordered by the GWR in 1946 was not delivered by its Swiss builders until 1950, but an English-built version appeared the following year. Despite BR deciding to build a fleet of steam locomotives rather than diesels (the first BR Standard locomotives appeared in 1951), production had hardly got into full swing before the 1955 Modernization Plan changed its policy to dieselization; several types appeared in 1958 and 1959, and this marked the beginning of the end of the steam locomotive.

Although steam was doomed, improvements continued, as it was anticipated that this mode of traction would still be used for many years to come. The drafting on 'Kings' and 'Castles' was improved in the mid-fifties,

enabling No. 6015 *King Richard III* to reach 108.5 mph on the 'Cornish Riviera Express' in 1955. In 1960 BR Standard class 9F 2–10–0s designed for heavy freight work were used on expresses in different parts of the country and reached an amazing 90 mph, for example between Leicester and Nottingham; en route from Cardiff to Paddington; and down Stoke Bank on the ex-Great Northern main line. When staff at BR headquarters heard of these exploits they quickly imposed a ban on such workings.

In the sixties engines often appeared well away from the routes on which they had previously been seen, such as 'Royal Scots' at Bristol together with ER class B1 4–6–0s and even on one occasion a class V2 2–6–2. ER class 01 and class 04 2–8–0s travelled well south of Birmingham and a class K3 2–6–0 penetrated to Milford Haven in west Wales. BR Standard class 6 4–6–2s, normally used only in

Organized by Southern Counties Railtours and hauled by rebuilt 'West Country' class Pacific No. 34108 *Wincanton,* this was the last BR steam-hauled train to use Brighton station. The date was 19.3.67. The next steam engine to visit Brighton was No. 34027 *Taw Valley* on 21.9.91 for the naming of Class 73/1 No. 73128 *O.V.S. Bulleid, CBE, CME Southern Railway 1937–1949.*

The 1967 'Southern Rambler Rail Tour' originated from Victoria, running to Brighton and Eastbourne before returning to London.

With the exception of Nos 34095/7/9/101/2/4, which were built at Eastleigh, all the 'West Country' and 'Battle of Britain' classes were built at Brighton Works, situated beyond platform 10 to the left of the photograph. The rebuilding of them took place at Eastleigh. *Wincanton* was withdrawn at the end of Southern steam on 9.7.67 and placed in store at Salisbury. It was towed to Buttigieg's at Newport and cut up in December 1968.

A.J. Fry Collection

Scotland and the north of England, travelled wider afield, at least one member being seen at Bristol and another at Newport. Bulleid Pacifics worked through to Birmingham on occasion from the Southern Region, while an ex-LMS 'Jubilee' appeared at Exeter.

The advent of the class 52 'Western' diesel-hydraulics in 1961 sounded the death knell of the 'Kings'. Although the Western Region was the first to become all-diesel, a move planned for the end of November 1965, the delayed demise of the Somerset and Dorset caused this to be postponed and the region retained its steam until the closure of Banbury shed on 3 October 1966. The last BR main-line steam engine ran in August 1968.

Most of the withdrawn steam engines were sold to scrap merchants who broke them up rapidly, but fortunately one firm, Woodham Brothers of Barry, did not do so immediately and many were eventually purchased from them and restored. A few engines were purchased direct from BR for preservation, while a few were saved for the National Collection, now part of the National Railway Museum.

The last days of steam coincided with the Beeching Report recommending the closure of many branch lines and numerous main-line country stations, so quite often a special train was run to mark the end of a branch line. Frequently the closure of a branch was the death warrant of the engines which worked it, for they were rarely needed elsewhere.

Good arguments can be put forward for and against the rapid scrapping of British locomotives, many of which were modern and could have continued in use for another twenty or thirty years, and enthusiasts were sad to see them go, for they marked the end of an era. Today we must be grateful that so many have once again been restored to working order.

A pristine 'Battle of Britain' class Pacific, No. 34050 *Royal Observer Corps*, of 70D (Basingstoke) climbs out of Dorking with the 'Wealdsman Rail Tour' on Sunday 13.6.65, organized by the Locomotive Club of Great Britain. Two months later the locomotive was withdrawn from service and cut up at Bird's, Morriston, Swansea. On the cabside of No. 34050 is a replica of the long-service medal of the ROC. To accommodate this, the triangular symbol indicating that BR water treatment was fitted to the locomotive had to be moved forward to a site below the figure 3 of the number.

A.J. Fry Collection

All 66,990 lb of tractive effort is being utilized as rebuilt 'Merchant Navy' class No. 35007 *Aberdeen Commonwealth* and No. 35008 *Orient Line* climb out of Weymouth with the return 'Southern Region Farewell to Steam' special to Waterloo on Sunday 2.7.67. No. 35007, without nameplates but with a smokebox numberplate, piloted the train as far as Bournemouth, where it was detached. Speeds in the last days of steam were often above average and on this occasion 88 mph was reached on the Down journey and 90 mph on the Up.

A.J. Fry Collection

With both connecting and coupling rods removed, 'Battle of Britain' class No. 34090 *Sir Eustace Missenden Southern Railway*, and 'West Country' class No. 34025 *Whimple* wait at Salisbury shed to be moved to their final destination, Cashmore's scrapyard. The rods were removed to free the motion and stored in the tender's coal bunker. With the nameplate holder removed, the three sand boxes are clearly visible on the running plate. The mechanical lubricators are sited between the front and middle sand boxes, and the clack valves supplying the boiler with water are mounted above them. When the Pacifics were rebuilt, additional weights were added to the centre driving wheels and these can be seen in his view, as can the brake rodding.

A.J. Fry Collection

'West Country' class No. 34018 *Axminster* in a siding at Bath on 19.2.68, en route to Cashmore's scrapyard. As was customary, the side rods have been removed for travel and placed in the tender. The cabside with the locomotive's number on has been vandalized.

Colin G. Maggs

A sad scene at Woodham's scrapyard in February 1967. Double-chimneyed No. 6024 *King Edward I* is in the foreground, with an 0–6–0PT and unrebuilt SR Pacific to the right, and another GWR 4–6–0 to the left. Fortunately, No. 6024 was not scrapped, and was eventually restored at the Didcot Steam Centre.

Colin G. Maggs Collection / W.H. Harbor